Making Friends
with the
Bible

To our spouses,
Betsy Baker Kilgore and
David A. Fraser

Making Friends

with the

Bible

Elouise Renich Fraser
and Louis A Kilgore

Foreword by Dorothy Jean Weaver

HERALD PRESS
Scottdale, Pennsylvania
Waterloo, Ontario

Library of Congress Cataloging-in-Publication Data
Fraser, Elouise Renich, 1943-
    Making Friends with the Bible / by Elouise Renich Fraser and
Louis A. Kilgore.
        p. cm
    ISBN 0-8361-3666-7
    1. Bible—Use. 2. Christian life—1960- I. Kilgore, Louis A.,
1955- . II. Title.
BS538.3.F735 1994
220'.07—dc20   94-3953
                                                                                 CIP

MAKING FRIENDS WITH THE BIBLE
Copyright © 1994 by Herald Press, Scottdale, Pa. 15683
    Published simultaneously in Canada by Herald Press,
    Waterloo, Ont. N2L 6H7. All rights reserved
Library of Congress Catalog Number: 94-3953
International Standard Book Number: 0-8361-3666-7
Printed in the United States of America
Book and cover design by Jim Butti

00 99 98 97 96 95 94 10 9 8 7 6 5 4 3 2 1

Contents

Foreword

This book is a delightful find! The authors speak simply and from the heart about their rediscovery of the Scriptures. As they tell of their own experiences with Bible study, they also invite the reader to join them in the ongoing journey of "making friends with the Bible."

We may have listened to Bible stories since childhood. We may have just discovered the Scriptures. We may dislike reading the Scriptures because we find them perplexing, problematic, or worn out. But no matter what our reaction to Scripture, this book is for us.

Making Friends with the Bible is both a gentle appeal and a hard-hitting exposé. What characterizes the book above all is its absolute honesty about the task of Bible study. The authors begin their discussion by exposing the many ways in which we hide from the Bible through blaming it, idolizing it, protecting it, distancing it.

In a second stage the authors reflect, often in surprising fashion, on the steps involved in a meaningful encounter with the Scriptures: "focus first on myself, not on the Bible"; "accept my limitations as good"; "accept the Bible just as it is"; "accept the reality of my distorted understanding"; "accept that the Bible won't always seem to be my friend"; "include others in the process"; "count on God's presence in this process."

Finally the authors open the pages of their respective journals and invite the reader to follow along as they think, feel, struggle, and celebrate their way through the study of three biblical texts—Luke 2:1-20, Jonah 1 and 2, and Romans 8:1-18. It is this willingness of the authors to be painfully honest about their own encounters with the Bible that gives their book its authority and its appeal.

Tucked away within these pages is a wealth of insights into the Scriptures themselves and into those of us who read them. One very basic insight has to do with our own self-awareness as we read the Scriptures. As the authors put it, "If I want to befriend the Bible, I can't treat it as though it were the only object of investigation. I must also investigate myself. I must be as honest and clear as I can about what I am bringing to the relationship today." In other words, who I am and the circumstances of my life have a great deal to do with how I view the Scriptures and what I find when I read them.

A second basic insight concerns our human limitations as we read the Scriptures. The authors put it this way:

> Our understanding of the Bible is limited by our experience of the world and of life. We've each seen a corner, but none of us has seen it all. Our experiences are invaluable resources in our study of the Bible. But they do not set limits for what the Bible may or may not mean. People who don't see it the way I see it aren't necessarily blind. They may never have seen what I have seen, just as I've never seen what they have seen.

Here is a strong call for humility as we read the Scriptures and a strong challenge to talk with each other as we interpret what we read.

A third basic insight relates to the character of the Scriptures themselves. On the one hand the authors call us to recognize the Bible's humanity.

> The Bible presents itself as the witness of human beings who are like we are, even though they live in different times and places. Like us, they have human limitations and live in a fallen world. Like us, they are learning to come out of hiding and trust God instead of their fears. To overlook the Bible's humanity is also to overlook their humanity.

On the other hand, to recognize the Bible's humanity does not mean that we deny its inspiration. As the authors affirm, "The written Word of God is inspired because God breathes life into its pages, today as well as yesterday."

But even more compelling than the authors' words about the task of Bible study is the example they provide as they study the Scriptures for themselves. There is an infectious excitement here born of the firm conviction that the Scriptures do indeed bring "good news" to humankind and that we will surely discover this good news as we apply ourselves faithfully to the task of Bible study. We need this kind of infection in the church.

—Dorothy Jean Weaver, professor
Eastern Mennonite Seminary
Harrisonburg, Virginia

Preface

This book is about our rediscovery of the Bible. It's about our excitement, our sense of wonder, and the healing of old wounds. It's about taking another look at the Bible, how we read it, and what we think it's saying. It's about our lives. And it's about God's grace.

We invite you to reconsider the Bible. It doesn't matter how long or how well you've known the Bible. It doesn't matter whether you identify yourself as a Christian or not, or how long it has been since you opened the Bible just because you wanted to. The Bible is good news for *all* people.

Over the years many of us have become less and less familiar with the Bible. We've lost whatever shared memory we may once have had of its contents. We've forgotten how to live with this book. Some of us have become increasingly willing to let go of pieces of the Bible because they don't seem to proclaim good news. Even people who defend the Bible and study it regularly often have unexpressed doubts and questions about the Bible.

Is the Bible *really* good news? Both of us grew up in homes saturated with the Bible through family Bible reading, Bible memorization, Bible quizzes, Bible songs, at least one Bible for each family member, books about the Bible, devotional guides to the Bible, Bible studies, vacation Bible school, hand-painted plaster of paris plaques containing Bible verses in every room of the house, and pencils engraved with "Thy Word is a lamp unto my feet."

Somewhere along the way all this good news began to sound like bad news. The Bible seemed to become primarily a book of law, a source of condemnation, a reminder of our many failures and inadequacies. Attempts to find lifegiving interpretations of old, familiar, but disturbing passages got bogged down in endless debates over technical questions. Was it worth the effort? It became easier to talk about the grace of God—and more difficult to talk about the grace of the Bible.

Several years ago we began talking together about our struggle to relate to the Bible. We made a few tentative connections between the way we treat each other and the way we treat the Bible. To our amazement, new worlds began opening up not just in the Bible, but in our lives. The key wasn't more education, better Bible translations, or less biased and more up-to-date commentaries. The key was *how we relate to the Bible.* Were we treating it as a friend? Or as an enemy?

Making Friends with the Bible is a report of what we've learned so far. It's written chiefly in the first person singular. With one exception, the final example in Part III, Elouise actually wrote the book. It is, nonetheless, the product of months and years of working together. We talked, Elouise wrote, Louis read and responded. We met and talked again, Elouise rewrote, Louis added more stories and illustrations, Elouise rewrote. We met and talked again.

The process was long, cumbersome, and costly. The telephone company didn't understand that we should have a discount. The forty-four miles between us seemed to go on forever. Sometimes we felt like quitting. But we knew the book was about more than reclaiming the Bible. It was about reclaiming pieces of ourselves and of God, pieces that had gotten lost along the way. So we just kept going.

As we proceeded, the book developed into three parts. In the first part we describe a problem that gets in our way when we relate to the Bible, keeping us from hearing its good news. In the second part we describe a seven-step process for making friends with the Bible. After each step is an exercise to help you put the step into practice. Accompanying each exercise, when appropriate, is an example from Elouise's journal to show what this looks like in practice. Part three contains several extended examples to demonstrate further how the process works. We've used the New Revised Standard Version for our examples but invite you to follow along in any standard version you prefer.

The stories and illustrations throughout the book come from both of us. Sometimes we've changed the identities of the actors. Some stories are personal. It would be useless to try to figure out who's who, since our lives are similar in many ways. Both of us come from Christian families, are male preacher's kids, have numerous siblings, and have gifted mothers who worked hard at home and in the church. We grew up in conservative Christian circles, attended church and Sunday school faithfully, graduated from Bible college and seminary, taught school, work today in Christian ministry, and are married with children. Instead of trying to identify us, we invite you to search for yourselves.

As we wrote this book we were immersed in family life

and the demands of seminary teaching and pastoral ministry. During this time Louis and Betsy welcomed their two youngest children into the world. Then, with their four children, they moved to another church and home, and Louis prepared for ordination as a Presbyterian minister. Elouise and David shared living space, a small kitchen, and two cars with their two young adult children. Elouise went through tenure review and two promotion reviews.

We were cheered at every step by our students, parishioners, colleagues, friends, and family. We are deeply grateful for their enthusiastic support, thoughtful and constructive feedback, and prayers for patient endurance. In particular, we thank our many friends at our primary communities of worship and service—Eastern Baptist Theological Seminary, Gladwyne Presbyterian Church, Sandy Ridge Community Church, and First Presbyterian Church of Ewing.

In the providence of God nothing is accidental. We acknowledge especially Perry Engle, who first suggested we might write a book together; Rouhle Tunley, who graciously shared his early enthusiasm for the subject matter and his expert editorial comments and questions; Lou Bamberg, who read a few pages and knew immediately what title to give the book; and Carol Schreck, who first showed a piece of the manuscript to Michael King at Herald Press.

Finally, we thank God for our spouses, Betsy and David. They have lived through the entire process with us, always believing that the book would be finished. We are grateful for their faithful presence. This book was written with them in view.

—*Elouise Renich Fraser*
Gladwyne, Pennsylvania
Louis A. Kilgore,
Ewing, New Jersey

PART I

The Problem of Hiding
from the Bible

Introduction

I don't remember how all the words went, but I'll never forget the setting—opening assembly in Sunday school and vacation Bible school. We stood reverently at attention, pledging allegiance first to the flag of the United States of America, then to the Christian flag, and finally to the Bible. Our voices rang out, "I pledge allegiance to the Bible, God's holy Word!" It was an honor to be one of the flag bearers. It was a far greater honor to stand between them, bearing the Bible in my hands. Obviously there were woven into that scene complex issues of church and state relations I wasn't aware of at the time. But what lingers beyond the complexities is the honor of bearing that Bible.

Then there was elementary school. It was a Christian school run by a church, and every year we were required to take a Bible course. We took Bible the way we took reading, writing, history, health, and arithmetic. We learned dozens of Bible stories and memorized long lists of kings and prophets and apostles. We recited whole chapters of the Bible by heart. We learned to find any verse in the Bible in two seconds flat.

Then there were mysteriously compelling rules about how *not* to treat your Bible. Never put it on the floor beside your desk. And never, ever, stack anything else on top of your Bible inside your desk!

The Bible isn't a book just like every other book. Even people who didn't grow up reading and studying the Bible seem to know the Bible is different. Whether we claim to live by its truths or not, we all want to make peace with this book. Most of us want to be friends with the Bible. Or at least to be known as people who are familiar with it.

Like a mysterious stranger, the Bible tantalizes us by showing up in movies, on TV, in Broadway shows, drama, novels, and even political speeches. No one seems to be able to leave it alone. And everyone seems to assume that everyone else knows its leading stories and themes.

It may seem strange, then, that many of us spend so little time actually reading the Bible itself. Maybe that's our way of admitting the truth about ourselves. It isn't that we don't care about the Bible, or that we don't want to know the Bible. It's much simpler than that. We just aren't sure how to do it. Not how to *read* the Bible, but how to *make friends* with the Bible.

The basic rule of friendship

We believe friendship with the Bible is possible for everyone. The only requirement is that you treat the Bible as a friend. This sounds easy, but many of us don't know how to go about it. Some of us have known the Bible a long time. We sing in church about how much we love it. We listen to sermons from it week after week. We may have memorized favorite verses and entire chapters, or preached and taught from it for years. But this may be deceiving.

A friend of mine spent days crying over the discovery that after fifteen years of marriage, he didn't know his wife very well. He had always believed he knew her better than she knew herself. He even amazed himself sometimes at how well he could read her mind! So when she divorced him and took up smoking and motorcycle riding, he was convinced she had gone crazy. He pursued her and tried to do her a favor by getting her back on what he thought was the right track. After many failures he had to admit he didn't know her well at all.

It's possible to spend years with someone, but miss knowing him or her as a friend. In the same way, it's possible to spend hours with the Bible, and miss knowing it as a friend. We may know many things about it. Perhaps there was a day when we knew it as a friend. But what about today? People who seem to know the most about the Bible may be as far away from it as people who don't seem to know much about it at all.

Sometimes we divide people into experts and nonexperts when it comes to knowledge about the Bible. But this may not be a helpful distinction. I remember my grandmother telling me over and over that an expert is only someone a long way from home. If you want to be an expert, just travel to another country. The people there will consider you an expert on the country you just left, even though they know nothing about your personal history.

People we think of as Bible experts may be able to quote chapter and verse on almost any topic. But they may also have difficulty describing the connection between the words on the page and their own lives. Or their relationship to the Bible may have become stale and dry. Perhaps they sense that something is missing, but they may be too embarrassed to admit it openly.

People who never think of themselves as experts on the Bible may have a similar problem. They may feel discouraged because there doesn't seem to be much connection between the Bible and their lives. They know the Bible is important, and sometimes they attend Bible studies. But they don't say much. They're afraid someone might ask them what the Bible says about something, or what they think it means. They wish they knew how to quote chapter and verse.

Somehow we've gotten the idea that making friends means spending hours and hours together, and knowing all there is to know about each other. Or enough so that you think you can read the other person's mind, or predict what he or she will do next. But the most basic rule of friendship isn't "Spend hours with each other," or "Gather as much information about each other as you possibly can." Instead, it's simply *"Accept each other just the way you are."* This means that if I want to make friends with other people, I must risk letting other people see me just as I am. And I must risk seeing them just as they are.

Friendship with the Bible is like friendship with each other. The most basic rule for making friends with the Bible isn't "Spend hours with the Bible," or "Gather as much information about it as you possibly can." Instead, it's simply, "Accept the Bible and yourself just the way you are." If I want to make friends with the Bible, I must risk being honest about myself while I'm reading it, and I must risk letting the Bible speak for itself.

The rule is simple. But we don't often keep it with the Bible for the same reason we don't often keep it with each other. We're afraid. Afraid to accept ourselves just the way we are.

Often we have good reasons. We're afraid to face what we're really thinking, or how we're really feeling, or what we would really like to be doing right now. We want to trust in God. But it's easier to trust in our fears. We're afraid of what might happen if the people we want to be friends with were to see us just as we are. And so we hide.

The problem of hiding

Recently I dropped by the home of a new church member. I had a paper that needed revision and was looking for advice. As I stood in the doorway, my new friend's next-door neighbor came by. During the introductions, it became painfully obvious my new friend didn't want his neighbor to discover he had recently joined a church. But it was almost impossible for him to explain my presence and my relationship to him without giving away the secret of his new involvement in the church. An uneasy silence developed. None of us felt comfortable standing there, looking at one another.

Hiding is a big problem in our friendships with each other. This shouldn't surprise us. One of the oldest stories about human beings is about hiding. Adam and Eve hid from each other and from God. Ever since the beginning we've been hiding from each other.

We move in and out of hiding constantly. We do it by turning attention away from ourselves and onto someone or something else. We do it by controlling when, where, and how much to let just the right people know what we're thinking or feeling. We're afraid to let other people see us as we are. We fear what the neighbors might think. Sometimes we think we don't have anything to offer.

Hiding is one of the things we do best in a fallen world. It isn't something some people do more than others. We *all* hide—men and women, young and old, rich and poor, extrovert and introvert, employed and unemployed, advertisers and consumers, misers and philanthropists, parents and children, students and teachers, pastors and congregations, Southerners and Northerners, pacifists and non-pacifists, Christians and Jews, black and white, North Americans and South Americans, people of every race, religion, and nationality. We are equally familiar with hiding.

Hiding is a survival tactic. It proclaims a bitter truth

about our world: human beings aren't always trustworthy. But hiding is also a tragic theme running through our lives. We hide from each other even though we long to be seen and accepted just as we are.

We don't leave the problem of hiding behind when we turn to the Bible. In its opening pages the Bible tells us hiding has deep roots in us personally and in our history with each other. The Bible is the story of human beings hiding from themselves, from each other, and from God.

But that's not all. If we take seriously our problem of hiding, we must acknowledge that hiding has also affected our relationship with the Bible itself. The way we relate to the Bible is part of our personal histories and part of our history with each other. If we want to work on our friendship with the Bible we must learn to recognize how we hide from it and take steps to change our behavior.

We don't usually think about ways our problem of hiding affects our relationship to the Bible. We may be convinced our biggest problems are lack of time or lack of information about the Bible. Maybe we're just hiding from it.

Hiding from
the Bible

There are blatant ways of hiding. Children are particularly good at this. They often announce loudly to their parents or to guests, "I'm going to hide now!" After they've done their best to conceal at least some parts of their bodies, you can ask what they're doing and they'll always say, "I'm hiding!" It's clear they're hiding, even though they're still semi-visible. It's also clear they want you to come looking for them.

Adults know from experience that in the church we have a lot to gain by staying on the friendly side of the Bible and pretending we're *not* hiding. So even though there are blatant forms of hiding, chances are we've learned over the years to cloak most of our hiding in subtleties. In fact, we may have become so subtle that we deceive not just the people around us but ourselves as well. We believe with all our hearts that we're friends with the Bible and that we have its best interests at heart.

In this chapter we're going to describe four ways we

sometimes hide from the Bible. Perhaps you'll think of others. One thing makes them all alike. They are ways of avoiding what the Bible wants us to see not just about ourselves, but about the Bible itself.

Blaming the Bible

Like the people with whom we live and work, the Bible doesn't always live up to our expectations. We say the Bible is indispensable if we're going to know who we are in relation to God and to each other. We've even heard people call it an exciting book. But when we finally pick it up and begin reading, it doesn't take long to remember why we don't read it more often.

When I was a child, I dreamed of playing the piano. I believed I would be really great at it if only I just sat down and did it. When I finally began my lessons I hoped to discover the truth of the old saying, "The hardest part is getting started." Instead, I discovered why I had waited so long to begin. Every time I put my fingers on the keyboard, I was reminded how difficult it is to learn to play well.

Reading the Bible is like playing the piano. We may open our Bibles thirty times, only to be reminded thirty times of why we've waited so long. So we close our Bibles, like closing the lid on a piano, and go into hiding. We hide by pointing to something about the Bible as the problem. We blame *it*, rather than facing the possibility that the problem lies in *us*. Whether we say the words or not, we believe it's the Bible's fault that it isn't everything we want it to be.

Most of us want the Bible to be easy to understand. Since it's an important book, you'd think it would be less complicated. But the Bible is never easy enough to understand, and talking about how hard it is to understand has become one of our favorite pastimes in church school and Bible study.

Contradictions seem to multiply as we read first one part of the Bible and then another. Wouldn't it be simpler if there were only one creation account, or just one gospel, or just one Testament? Then there are those mysterious words and symbols that even the scholars argue about. We tell ourselves we would read the Bible more often if only it weren't so complex.

Sometimes the Bible seems to put us in a bind. It says we're to love our neighbors, but we're also to hate our families and friends for the gospel's sake. It says we're to obey God, but we're also to obey our parents and our political leaders. It says we're to trust God alone for our salvation, but we're also to do good works. It says we're not supposed to kill each other, but then it seems to celebrate when God's people kill their enemies. We tell ourselves we wouldn't have so much trouble following the Bible's teachings if only the Bible weren't so confusing.

Then there's the other side. For some of us, the problem with the Bible isn't that it's too complex. The real problem is that it's so naive.

Recently my mother asked me to look at an old trunk in her attic. It was a simple, plain trunk, scarred and badly damaged from many years of use. Was it too far gone to be worth restoring? Was it interesting enough to be worth anything today?

Sometimes we ask the same questions about the Bible. Perhaps we really don't need it since it has limited value as an antique and seems too unsubstantial to be of any practical use in today's world. It just isn't sophisticated enough. If the Bible is going to be relevant, it needs to show awareness of issues that are important right now. To some of us the Bible seems so naive and out of touch with what we need in our enlightened age that it just makes matters worse.

For example, if it weren't for all that male dominance in

the Bible, women might not have such difficulty being accepted as full partners in life. If it weren't for all those war stories and that warrior God in the Old Testament, peacemaking might be easier. If it weren't for all those teachings about respect for authority, the poor and the powerless might not be exploited nearly so much. The Bible seems more than naive; it seems blind to its own biases.

We blame the Bible for our confusion, anger, and disillusionment. We're so convinced there's something wrong with the Bible that only rarely do we consider whether the problem might be something about *us*. We act as though we would be able to understand the Bible fully or see its relevance immediately if only it presented itself differently. We forget that even if all the problems we think we see in the Bible were resolved, we would still have to deal with the way our own limitations and problems affect our understanding.

The issue isn't whether the Bible is easy enough to understand or relevant enough to our times. Rather, it's whether we're willing to admit there may be something about us that makes it difficult to understand the Bible.

We already know our understanding of any book is related to who we are at the time we read it. To children, *Alice in Wonderland* is a fantasy about funny people who have strange but enjoyable experiences. The tales of Brer Rabbit and Brer Bear offer endless amusement and more than enough imaginary creatures to fill a child's daydreams. But to the adults who wrote these stories and to adults who read them accordingly, they are stinging commentaries on social conditions and human behavior. Instead of entertainment for children, they are graphic descriptions of life in a fallen world. When we grow up what was simple becomes hard, not because the story changed, but because we changed.

The Bible isn't a simple book. But neither is it inaccessible, incoherent, or unintelligible. If making friends with the Bible is like making friends with another person, then I will discover how to listen to it and how it makes sense only over a period of time. The task of understanding is never finished—not just because the Bible is challenging, but because changes in me will always affect the way I relate to this text.

Idolizing the Bible

Strategies for hiding are like layers of an onion. Peel back one layer and you'll find another. When we blame the Bible for being difficult or irrelevant, it's often a signal we've already been hiding from it by idolizing it. Instead of accepting this friend just as it is, we've set it up as though it were God. When it doesn't deliver what we want, we point a finger of blame at *it* instead of at our own false expectations.

Our expectations about what the Bible will do for us know no bounds. Every time we had a fire drill in elementary school, our teachers reminded us of one unbreakable rule. Don't go back for anything! Even in freezing temperatures we were to head straight for the nearest exit without going back for *anything*. Not even coats or hats.

In Sunday school we learned a different rule. No one ever said it was a rule. Somehow we just figured it out. Every time our Sunday school teachers asked us what we would grab as we fled our burning houses, or what we would go back to rescue, we had the answer down cold. The Bible! Everything else could be replaced.

We talk a lot about how much the Bible means to us, and how we could never get along without it. It sounds as though we respect and love the Bible deeply. But we may be setting it up to disappoint us.

Sometimes we do this by expecting the Bible to tell us what we should think, or how we should feel, or what we should do in a particular situation. Some people consider the Bible a resource for predicting what's going to happen in world politics. Others turn to it for less global but often more pressing problems, like how to raise a teenager, or which job to take, or whether to go to college.

The problem isn't that we turn to the Bible for guidance about how we should live, or about our involvement in world affairs. Rather, it's that we sometimes consult the Bible as though it were a book of ready-made answers. We want it to lay everything out clearly and unambiguously so that all we have to do is take notes and memorize them. We expect it to be an easy teacher. We want it to absolve us from the hard work of figuring things out for ourselves, and from taking the risk of making our own choices and then living with the consequences.

At other times we idolize the Bible by expecting it to excuse us from the work of relating to each other and to God. We think that if we become thoroughly acquainted with everything the Bible has to say about relationship, we won't have to risk it in real life. If the Bible will just tell us the principles of right relationship, we won't have to live through the reality of our fears, our foolishness, or our fallenness.

Many of us have participated in Bible conferences and retreats that focus on family relationships. We know too well the depression of returning home and discovering little connection between the excitement of what we heard or studied and what happens at home. Some of us would like to spend our entire lives in Bible conferences and retreats, focusing on what the Bible says relationships ought to be like—rather than going home and living with them just as they are. We want the teaching of the Bible to save us from the discomfort and agony of what happens at home.

We also idolize the Bible when we expect it to fight our

battles for us. We expect it to be on our side, support our causes, and even demolish our enemies. We bring the Bible in as a third party in our relationships, using it as a weapon of control or as a tool to fix other people. When I was a child, I wondered whether everyone else's parents had the same favorite Bible verse as mine: "Children, obey your parents." This was followed by a close second, "Do all things without murmuring or complaining."

Instead of looking our friends or enemies in the eye and saying what *we* think or feel, we often quote the Bible or appeal to one of its teachings. We expect it always to be on *our* side, which means, of course, the side of justice, truth, and good behavior!

Finally, we idolize the Bible when we expect it *not* to be human. When we discover difficulties in it, our distress betrays our expectation that the Bible will have no flaws or imperfections.

At the Christian college I attended, one of the professors always began his introductory course with an invitation. Any student who believed the Bible had no mistakes in it at all could come by his office. He would demonstrate why he himself didn't believe this. It was a shocking invitation. No one took him up on it, even though most of us were secretly disturbed by the possibility that the Bible might be flawed in any way.

My professor spared us the embarrassment of coming to his office and gave his demonstration anyway. It went like this. Everyone knows that only cows chew their cud. But Leviticus 11:6 says the rabbit chews its cud! Even though the explanation for this was simple and understandable, some of us were distressed. It seemed *God* had just been called into question.

We expect the Bible to be full and complete, the perfect image of God. We expect it to answer all our questions, as though it were the mind of God. Our excitement about the Bible being made available to people for the first time may betray our belief that God isn't present until the Bible is present. Sometimes we confuse the presence of this book with the presence of God.

But the Bible isn't God. It's a witness God has chosen to use just as it is.

The Bible isn't a weapon on my side, against my friends and enemies. It's a witness that stands on everyone's side by speaking the truth to everyone.

The Bible isn't a substitute for the risky business of relationship. It's a witness to just how difficult relationships are in this fallen world.

And the Bible isn't an easy teacher. It's a witness inviting us to take seriously our own responsibility for what we think, feel, and do.

We set the Bible up as though it were God in order to make things easier for ourselves. Kermit the frog sings everyone's song when he laments, "It's not easy being green." It's not easy being human, and it's understandable when we're tempted to take shortcuts. The tragedy is that by taking shortcuts we miss seeing not just ourselves as we really are, but the Bible as it really is.

Protecting the Bible

In the very first Bible study I ever taught, I invited people to listen to Luke 9:57-62 as though no one but Luke were speaking to us. The verses talk about following Jesus without going home to bury dead family members or even to say good-bye. It was a difficult Bible study, and most people didn't come back the following week. I wasn't sure I wanted to either. Luke's words seemed too harsh, and we couldn't find a way to connect them with the way we live every day.

Some of us fear nothing more than seeing the Bible as it really is. This fear becomes the occasion for another way of hiding from the Bible. We're convinced the Bible needs our help, so we set out to protect it. We set ourselves up to defend and fix it. We treat it as though it were a junior partner incapable of entering fully into conversation with us and ignorant of the truth about itself.

We protect the Bible from criticism and disrespect by always saying nice things about it. Even though we may be angry, confused, or even bored with it, we don't admit this. We think that because it's a holy book, it wouldn't be able to survive the truth about our thoughts and feelings toward it. We have a list of questions we never ask about the Bible, since it might appear to be no longer trustworthy. We try to promote positive feelings toward the Bible and to demonstrate its relevance by quoting favorite verses or passages, even though we're not sure how they connect with our lives.

Sometimes we protect the Bible from being misunderstood by ignoring parts of it. We usually study, teach, and preach passages we find clear and helpful. Parts of the Bible seem bizarre and strange, so we just avoid them as much as possible. Most are in the Old Testament. Perhaps we're afraid the Bible might be mistaken for a book about sex and violence. Or we're afraid the clarity of the gospel might be obscured by the mysterious signs and visions in the Revelation to John.

When we don't find the guidance we think we need for today, we sometimes protect the Bible by making excuses for it. We act as though the Bible were an unenlightened child, beautiful in its simplicity, but not yet fully versed in the affairs of this world. We respect the Bible, but we wouldn't want anyone to have the wrong idea about the Bible's ability to speak to the issues of our day. After all, isn't the Bible tied to particular times and cultures? And don't we live in a far more complex world than any found in the Bible? Better to lower our expectations than to risk being disappointed or even misled.

Finally, we protect the Bible by trying to fix it. We take it upon ourselves to explain what *we* think it meant to say. Sometimes this means rearranging the text itself or even omitting pieces that don't fit, so it makes better sense from our point of view. It may also mean that instead of letting discrepancies stand, we try to resolve them so that the text says what we think it really meant to say all along. Or we may fix it by taking the sting out of its hard sayings. Surely Jesus didn't really mean we should leave our families for the sake of the Gospel.

Protection is a boomerang. We may think we're protecting the Bible, but we're actually protecting it in order to protect ourselves.

We say nice things about the Bible because we're afraid we might not survive the Bible's criticism of us. Or because we fear someone might discover that the Bible doesn't connect with our lives at all.

We ignore certain parts of the Bible because we're afraid we might be asked to say what we think about them.

We make excuses for its seeming simplemindedness because we're afraid we'll appear simpleminded for taking it seriously.

And we fix it because we don't want anyone to see how much it disturbs us just the way it is.

Distancing the Bible

The last way we hide from the Bible may be the easiest of all, especially in the church. The dynamics of distancing are simple. We hide from what the Bible wants us to see by denying that the world of the Bible has anything to do with us. What happens in its pages is foreign to what we think, what we feel, and how we conduct ourselves in our world.

By far the most efficient way to distance the Bible is to avoid it completely. Avoid reading it, listening to sermons from it, talking about it, even thinking about it. That way it's clear. The world of the Bible is not our world.

But if we're going to survive in the world of the church, we can't afford to be this obvious. So over the years, we've learned to read the Bible as though it were a book about *other* people.

Sometimes we read it as a book about all those strange people living in their strange worlds way back in Bible times. It's the story of *their* sin and *their* inability to trust God and get along with each other. Their sin practically leaps off the pages at us.

We read about Adam and Eve. Then we say, "I can't believe they had all those advantages, then blew it! I wish God would put *me* in the Garden of Eden!"

We read in the book of the Judges about the slaughter of hundreds of innocent women, children, and men. We gasp in horror and say, "I can't believe how violent people were back then!"

We read about the nine lepers who didn't come back to thank Jesus for healing them. We shake our heads and say, "I can't believe how ungrateful they were!"

We read about Peter and James and John quarreling, and we say, "I can't believe how obsessed those men were with which of them would sit closest to Jesus in the kingdom of heaven!"

Or we read about the crowds crying "Hosanna" on one day, and "Crucify him" on the next, and we say, "I can't believe how fickle and blind those people were!"

We turn away from this sad and sometimes shocking spectacle, thankful we are not like other people—swindlers, unjust, adulterers, or even like tax collectors. To those of us who are confident in ourselves that we are righteous, and view others with contempt, Jesus told the parable of the Pharisee who went up into the temple to thank God that he was not like other people.

But it's too late. We are already those people. Their sins are *our* sins; their world is *our* world. Yet we won't see how this could be until we risk coming out of hiding from the Bible.

What about the people we admire in the Bible? Sadly, most of us have learned to distance them as well. They too are strange people living in a distant time and place. Their goodness practically leaps off the pages at us, and we're convinced we could *never* be like they are.

We read about Noah building an ark even though it hadn't begun to rain. Or Abraham and Sarah leaving their home without knowing where they were going. Or Ruth returning with Naomi to Bethlehem without knowing how they would get along as widows. Or Mary accepting the angel's announcement that she had been chosen by God to conceive and bear a son who would be named Jesus. Or blind Bartimaeus crying out and making a nuisance of himself in order to get Jesus' attention. Or Jesus on the cross asking God to forgive his enemies.

We read these stories and say, "I could *never* have that much faith!" Because we hide from the Bible, we don't see that we are also like people we admire in the Bible. We've already been given everything they were given. God has given us, as God gave them, direction and strength for life, in this world. But hiding from the truth about ourselves has blinded us to the truth about how God is already present in our lives.

There's one other way we distance the Bible. Instead of reading it as a book about all those people back then, we read it as a book about all those people around us right now. Just as we're blind to our own goodness, we're blind to theirs as well.

When we first meet people, their shortcomings usually stand out in our minds. No wonder many of us are afraid to meet new people. We expect them to focus on *our* shortcomings in the same way we focus on theirs. It's always a surprise to find people who don't operate this way.

I remember my first appointment with the supervisor for my seminary internship. I had developed a nasty habit of being late, and this was no exception. I remember my shock when I arrived but my supervisor didn't seem to notice I was late, even though she had been waiting for me. I was so uncomfortable that I asked her later in the interview whether she had noticed I was late. Yes, she had noticed. But she said no more about it. Only later did I realize she was so happy I had arrived that she didn't have time to focus on my shortcomings!

When we open the Bible, the sins of people with whom we live and work practically leap off the pages at us. We aren't children anymore, but hide-and-seek is still one of our favorite games. We hide from what the Bible is saying about us, and seek out someone else who needs to hear all about it. We listen to the sermon or the Bible lesson, and check to make sure all the right people are present. We may even preach the sermon or teach the lesson, and look around to make sure everyone who needed to hear this came today.

A young minister had recently become pastor of a country church. In the church was a very kind and supportive deacon who always took time to comment on the sermon. After a few weeks the young minister began to notice a disturbing pattern. No matter what else he said as he shook the preacher's hand, the deacon always ended by saying, "Well, it was a good sermon. They sure needed to hear that one!"

One winter morning it snowed so hard that only the minister and the deacon arrived for the worship service. Seeing a chance to make his point, the minister decided to go ahead and preach the sermon to his deacon. At the end of the service, the deacon greeted the pastor with his customary kindness and then said, "Well, it was a good sermon. Too bad they didn't come to hear it!"

We've become highly skilled at listening for what other people need to hear from the Bible. It's amazing how often what I think the Bible is saying to them is exactly what I think they need to hear! And it's equally amazing how close I feel I am to the Bible when I do this, even though I'm hiding from it.

The Bible isn't about other people. This may sound ridiculous, since the Bible seems to be talking about other people from beginning to end. It seems to be *their* story, the story of how God interacts with *them*. And it is. But that's only part of the truth.

The Bible is also the story of *my* life. In fact, until I understand how it's *my* story, I won't begin to understand how it's the story of anyone else's life. These things weren't written so I could distance myself from other people, past *or* present. Rather, they were written so I would know not just about other people in their strange worlds, but about myself in my strange world. The Bible invites me to see that *their* story is *my* story.

The Bible Isn't Your Enemy

The Bible is the story of our lives. This could be a problem, since most of us hate being reminded of what we're really like. We hate hearing our own voices on tape, or seeing ourselves on TV or in home movies. We have the same fear of seeing ourselves in the Bible. We're afraid the Bible will be the complete, unabridged version of "This Is Your Life." It will remind us once again of how many times we've disappointed ourselves and the people we most love and care about. It will magnify our faults and shortcomings, increase our guilt and shame, and pass deservedly harsh judgment on us.

A few years ago a couple came to me for premarital counseling. During one of our sessions I asked them to take a standard test. It would reveal something about each partner's personality, and where they might be alike and different. The woman agreed, but the man refused to take the test. He said he didn't want to look too closely at their relationship. He just wanted to discover it by surprise. He was sure the test would take all the fun out of it.

We don't like to look too closely at the Bible. We're afraid it might take all the fun out of our lives. Some of us have good reason to fear. Parts of the Bible have been used against us in misleading, manipulative, and openly hostile ways.

When I was growing up my parents used Bible stories to try to control my behavior. Other parents used the story of Santa Claus the same way, but Bible stories were obviously superior. Not only was there a seemingly endless supply, but you could use them all year long. Best of all, they were *true*. Of all the stories interpreted to me as a child, none was as powerful as the story of Adam and Eve.

Adam and Eve

According to the story of Adam and Eve as I learned it, God watches over all of us children, keeping track of who's been naughty and nice. In my family being nice usually meant keeping all the rules, being polite to everybody, and not making too much noise. Like Santa, God was the ever-present, all-seeing eye of the adult authority figures in my life. Especially when their backs were turned, or when they left the room for a few minutes. The story warned us not to be disobedient children like Adam and Eve. It put more than a little fear into our hearts, since God sees us even when we're hiding.

The story of Adam and Eve is one of the best known and most influential stories in the Bible. It is also one of the most misused and mistreated stories of all time. By silencing parts of it, we've managed to turn its good news into bad news. More precisely, we've managed to turn its good news about *all* of us into good news for only *some* of us. This means bad news for the rest of us.

The Bible is good news for *everyone*—children as well as parents, women a well as men, oppressors as well as oppressed. That doesn't mean it always sounds like good news. However, if our interpretations sound like good news or feel like painful news for only *some* of us, then we haven't listened carefully enough. We're still in our hiding places.

There are things the Bible is dying to tell us. Things that are good news for everyone. What's more, the Bible doesn't make us wait till later to find out what they are. It announces them right in its opening pages. The story of Adam and Eve isn't just a preface, getting us ready to hear the good news later. It *is* the good news. The same good news the Bible wants us to hear on every page. But we'll never hear it until we stop hiding from the Bible and learn to let it speak for itself. Especially through details we may have overlooked because we thought we already knew what it said.

We believe our ability to hear the good news in the story of Adam and Eve is connected to our ability to hear it in the rest of the Bible. It's also connected to the way we understand the stories of our personal lives, as well as our histories with each other. In addition, the story of Adam and Eve clarifies the direction we must take if we are to stop hiding from the Bible and learn to let it speak for itself.

We invite you to consider several discoveries we've made in the story of Adam and Eve. We had either overlooked or taken them for granted, because we thought we already knew what the text said. These discoveries invite us to see the story of Adam and Eve, along with the entire Bible, in ways we weren't taught to see them.

Human limitations

Our first discovery is deceptively simple: *Adam and Eve were limited as individuals in the same ways we are limited.* We sometimes imagine that they were unlimited, even though the story never says this. It isn't difficult to imagine some of their limitations. For example, they had to eat and sleep, and they needed clean air and fresh water, just as we do.

But we're talking about less obvious limitations. For example, just like us, Adam and Eve couldn't walk on water. They couldn't do more than one thing at a time. Or live more than one day at a time. Like us, each had only two hands and one pair of eyes. They could be in only one place at a time. They got around by putting one foot in front of the other. No eyes in the backs of their heads. No ability to read minds or to fulfill their hearts' desires by simply wishing for them. They had a limited number of hours each day. Things left undone when they went to sleep at night were still waiting for them the next morning. They weren't royal visitors to the Garden of Eden. They were the gardeners.

If we pass too quickly over the extent and nature of Adam and Eve's human limitations, we'll miss the significance of the next point, which is our next discovery. *Adam and Eve's human limitations were good.* They weren't tragic flaws in a pair of otherwise perfect creatures. Neither Adam nor Eve was commanded to overcome, transcend, or get rid of them. They weren't even named as the cause of Adam or Eve's sin.

We often think of Adam and Eve before the Fall as perfect specimens of humanity. This usually means they weren't bothered by whatever happens to be bothering us today. Take, for example, their human understanding. We like to think that before the Fall their understanding was unlimited. If there was something they didn't understand, it was simply because they hadn't yet thought it over.

But according to Genesis, neither Adam nor Eve had unlimited understanding. In fact, they were tempted in relation to things they *couldn't* understand. God looked at Adam and Eve with their limited understanding and pronounced them good.

The serpent looked at them and set out to convince them they should be able to understand as God does. The serpent wanted them to believe their limited understanding was bad and needed to be overcome. In an ironic move, the serpent, wise in the ways of human nature but not in the ways of God, offered Adam and Eve salvation from a need they didn't have.

The retail business has taken a lesson or two from the serpent. It seems that every day we hear of a cure for an ailment we didn't even know we had. It's always a relief to find that in the very instant the problem is identified, the cure is already on the market. Just think of the years of social humiliation we've all been spared because pharmaceutical companies told us at the same time about halitosis *and* mouthwash!

In the story of Adam and Eve, the Bible proclaims good news: human limitations are *good*. For example, it is good that none of us can see into the future or beyond the horizon. We sometimes act as though our limitations were a sad and sorry result of the Fall, or as though some of us had no limitations at all. But according to the story of Adam and Eve we are *all* limited. And our limitations are deeply rooted in the goodness of our humanity. The Bible never puts us down because of limitations.

Our need for human relationship

Just as we like to think Adam and Eve had no limitations before the Fall, so we like to think that before the Fall everything in the universe was good. We forget that when God looked at creation, not everything God saw was good. It wasn't good that Adam was alone, even though Adam was God's good creation.

Sometimes we imagine Adam's problem was loneliness. But according to Genesis, the problem was that Adam was alone. Adam needed another human being, one suitable for him. When God created Eve and brought her to Adam, God demonstrated it wouldn't be good for Eve to be alone, either. Eve needed a suitable companion. The discovery is simple: *Adam and Eve were limited by their need for human relationship.* Neither of them could make it alone.

Pop songs of the last few decades have celebrated being out there on my own, being a rock, doing it my way. But according to the story of Adam and Eve it isn't good to live as though we were alone in this world. One isolated being, male or female, isn't yet fully human. Like Adam and like Eve, we are needy because we can't make it on our own. We cannot survive without other people. We're limited by our need for human relationship.

This too is a *good* limitation. Sometimes we think our need for other human beings is a shameful, regrettable, or even sinful result of the Fall. We act as though we should be able to get along fine by ourselves. We apologize for intruding on other people's time. We would rather get by on our own than ask for help. But our need for human relationship is built right into the structure of the universe. We can't choose to take it or leave it. It's already deeply rooted in us as a good part of our humanity.

The creation of Eve marks the beginning of human relationship. From Adam and Eve we have inherited a longing for significant relationships with other people. One of the good gifts of creation is our need for other humans in our lives. Without this gift we would never experience the miracle of being drawn to other people or the wonder of discovering people suitable for us. In fact, our discovery of these people is a sign of God's involvement in our lives, just as it was for Adam and Eve.

Discovering suitable friends and companions doesn't mean our longing for significant human relationships will vanish. These people aren't in our lives to take away this gift of creation. They are there to remind us of God's involvement in our lives. In fact, we get into trouble when we imagine someone out there can or should meet our need so fully that we'll never long for another human relationship.

Sometimes we expect certain people always to be there for us. We don't say it out loud, but we expect them to deny their human limitations and their need for their own human relationships. At the heart of every abusive relationship lies the expectation that another human being can be a perfect or at least near-perfect companion, filling our physical, emotional, spiritual, or intellectual longings.

We have a difficult time accepting people whose human limitations and need for human relationship are just like our own. Sadly, we don't always want another *human* being in our lives. We really want a god or a goddess to make us happy, and solve all our problems.

I was on the fifth floor of a hospital, waiting impatiently for the elevator to stop at every floor before it finally stopped at mine. As I paced back and forth, I could hear a heated conversation between a doctor and the husband of a seriously ill elderly patient. The doctor had just signed a release so the woman could return home. Her husband was enraged. The doctor explained several times over that the patient had refused further treatment, and had every right to do so. But the man's rage continued. The argument went on as though the two of them were seated in a private office. But it was all embarrassingly public.

Finally the elevator arrived. The doctor stepped in with me, and the door closed on the painful anger of this husband and caretaker who had run out of options. The doctor leaned against the wall of the elevator and sighed. He said, "Whatever degree you get in life, get a degree in human beings! They love to diagnose their own needs and name their own cures. Then they get angry when life doesn't meet their expectations. People don't pay me to do what I can; they pay me to do what they want *God* to do!"

In this fallen world we're often treated as more than human or less than human. The story of Adam and Eve lets us know we're entitled to something better. We're entitled to *human* relationships. In fact, we witness to our God-given need for human relationships whenever we make choices that express our longing for suitable friends and companions. This doesn't mean perfect or even near-perfect relationships. It means relationships in which we work together to accept our individual limitations as good and to acknowledge our need for each other just as we are—not as we wish we were or think we ought to be.

Adam and Eve's sin

Human life as we know it began when Adam and Eve chose not to accept their limitations as good, including their need for each other. We often read this story as though Adam and Eve's sin was disobedience. But according to the account in Genesis, *Adam and Eve's sin was more complicated than simple disobedience to God's command.* True, God commanded them not to eat from the tree of the knowledge of good and evil. And they did it anyway. But their sin began long before they committed any outward act of disobedience.

Adam and Eve's sin began in their hearts—when they hid from the goodness of their limited knowledge. It began when they chose not to accept this limitation and accepted instead the temptation to transcend it. Eating the forbidden fruit was a small, seemingly irrelevant act. But it betrayed their belief that they would be happier without their limited knowledge. This seemingly harmless act was a sign they were already hiding from the goodness of their humanity. Then, having eaten the fruit, they hid again. This time they hid from God and from each other. Hiding from the truth about themselves led to even more hiding.

God didn't test Adam and Eve by issuing an arbitrary command or by setting up an artificial boundary. Instead God gave them an invitation. God asked whether they were willing to find contentment, fulfillment, and life itself in what God had given them. Could they find joy through what God had offered them individually, in each other, in the Garden, and in God's own presence with them?

God didn't give Adam and Eve just barely enough, then tell them they would just have to make do. Nor did God create them with unmet needs and longings so they could sit around and act like martyrs the rest of their lives. Rather, God gave Adam and Eve *more* than they needed for life in the Garden, including their longing for something beyond themselves. Then God invited them to discover that what God had already given them was indeed more than enough to fulfill even their deepest desires.

Sometimes people read this story as judgment on Eve for choosing to act independently. The story then becomes a warning to everyone—but especially women—about the danger of becoming active participants in life. Yet Eve's sin wasn't the choice to act on her own. Nor was it her feeling of being limited, or her discontent. Like Adam, Eve was created with limitations and longings. The Garden was a setting of abundance, but not so Adam and Eve would never have any longings or unfulfilled needs. Rather, the Garden was an invitation to believe that God had indeed provided more than enough. When needs were unmet, the Garden offered an abundance of ways to meet those needs. All Adam and Eve had to do was make responsible choices to take care of their needs.

Eve felt limited because she *was* limited. She longed for something more because God *gave* her that longing. Her decision to act to fill her longing wasn't sinful. The problem was acting in a certain way. She denied the goodness of her limited knowledge and chose the one way God had said would mean death. So did Adam.

The story of Adam and Eve isn't an invitation to blame them for our present situation. It's an invitation to look into the mirror and see ourselves. God extends to us the same invitation God extended to them. Our problem isn't simply that we disobey God's commands. It's that we refuse to accept God's invitation.

God invites us to accept our human limitations and to discover in what God has given us more than enough to satisfy our hearts' desires. Instead we try to get around and beyond our limitations, including our need for human relationships. We pretend we don't have these limitations. Worse, we come to believe that God has withheld from us what would truly fulfill our deepest desires. Like Adam and Eve, we demonstrate our belief that we can see more clearly than God sees. We believe we know better than God what we need, and how to get it.

Adam and Eve and God

I'll never forget my excitement when I first realized the opening chapters of Genesis aren't just the story of Adam and Eve. In fact, there isn't a story of Adam and Eve in the Bible at all! *What we call the story of Adam and Eve is, in fact, the story of Adam and Eve and God.*

I've always thought of the story of Jesus as the story of God with us. And it is. But so are all the other stories in the Bible. What we call the story of Cain and Abel is, in fact, the story of Cain and Abel and *God.* So is the story of Abraham and Sarah, Hagar and Sarah, Jacob and Esau, Ruth and Naomi, Esther and Ahasuerus, Mary and Joseph, Jesus and Mary Magdalene, and even Jesus and Judas. God is the third party in all these stories, present even when not named or openly acknowledged.

Sometimes we think of God as someone we can

choose to invite or not into our relationships. Often at wedding ceremonies and infant dedications the minister urges new couples and new parents to invite God to be an unseen partner in all they do. The idea of making room for God makes sense, especially since many of us feel guilty about not making room in our busy lives for the people we say we love.

It's true. We need God in our relationships if we are going to survive life together. But according to Genesis, God isn't a presence Adam and Eve can choose to live with or without. Rather, God is already present, even before the beginning. Without God, Adam and Eve wouldn't be there at all.

God is the only character in the story who is present not just before the beginning but also in the middle and even after Adam and Eve are gone. God begins their life together and God keeps it going. God alone knows what they need and what is best for them. God keeps on seeking them out when they hide. God doesn't side with one of them against the other but makes clothes for both, then goes with them in their life together outside the Garden.

God's presence is the first truth that touches all human reality. God doesn't wait for us to decide whether we would feel comfortable with God in the story. God is already with us.

The Bible wants us to see from the very beginning that God is with us. It also invites us to discover not ahead of time, but in the way things unfold, that *God is ultimately in control of what happens next.* Adam and Eve are not in control. We like to imagine that for one brief moment Adam and Eve held within their hands the destiny of the entire human race. But according to Genesis, that kind of power belongs to God alone. Adam and Eve had power. But their power was limited. And like their other limitations, this too was a *good* limitation. It meant Adam and Eve didn't have the capability of ruining the entire human race. When Adam and Eve sinned, creation did *not* fall back into formless chaos.

Perhaps we give Adam and Eve so much destructive power because we like to think we also hold in our hands the key to other people's destiny. But the story of Adam and Eve is the story of God holding this key. Not the serpent, not Eve, and not Adam. In a reversal of what we might expect, God's response communicates that this is incredibly serious, but it isn't the end of the world.

When God covers Adam and Eve, God signals they shouldn't make their sin more powerful than it is. God is in control, not their sin. Their sin, which is also our sin, is deep. But it isn't as powerful as we like to think it is. God can use anything in this world to advance the purposes of God, even our sin of hiding.

God's control

Sometimes we think of God's control the way we think of puppets on strings. This may be one of our worst fears—not just about God but about ourselves. Yet we don't usually imagine God behind the scenes controlling our every twitch, so that the only alternative would be for us to collapse into lifeless heaps. We're more likely to think of God's control the way we think of parental oversight. God gives us a certain amount of space in which to move, then watches vigilantly from the sidelines. That way God can intervene if necessary and set us straight, or even rescue us from disaster.

But the story of Adam and Eve offers another picture of God's control. Instead of hovering over Adam and Eve, God sets them free. God takes the risk of being seen, misunderstood, ignored, and even rejected. Setting Adam and Eve free doesn't mean withdrawing from them and just letting things take their course. Rather, it means *God chooses to participate fully with them, living not just with their good limitations, but with their attempts to deny these limitations.* God sets them free, but God doesn't abandon them.

We often talk about how important it is to respond to God. God calls; we are to answer. God speaks; we're to obey. But according to the story of Adam and Eve, God also responds to *us*. God doesn't simply take the initiative of creating the universe and then become a spectator, or a third party waiting passively for our response. In fact, God's control is seen most clearly in God's free response to Adam and Eve, not in some imagined script God prepared ahead of time for them to follow.

God follows Adam and Eve. God works through their free activity instead of doing their work for them "the right way." God doesn't go back to the beginning to create a new, undistorted universe. God doesn't return Adam and Eve to the way they were. Nor does God bring in some outside solution to the problem of their sin of hiding.

Instead God works from within the world as God created it, revealing to Adam and Eve what they have already been given. God's love for Adam and Eve is visible not just when God clothes them, but from the very beginning when God first sets them free. Ironically, when God is in control, it may seem God isn't in control at all.

After the Fall

Our final discovery is that *even though Adam and Eve's limitations were distorted by sin, God accepted them just as they were.* After the Fall Adam and Eve presented a sad and sorry picture. Their limited sight had become distorted. They no longer saw God as the good Creator but as the one ultimately responsible for this mess. They no longer saw each other as God's good creatures, but as accomplices worthy only of suspicion and distrust. And they were no longer willing to be seen by each other or by God, but became self-conscious and tried to hide. The reversal is dramatic and tragic.

No wonder we often read the closing verses of the story as though God were passing harsh judgment on them. Adam and Eve have lost their innocence. They must now suffer the consequences and be driven from the Garden. They've demonstrated to God and to each other that they aren't always trustworthy. In their responses to God's questions, they've revealed what they really think about God and about each other. They blame God and they resent each other.

As if that weren't enough, God has just described the painful consequences that await each of them. Only now does the magnitude of their sin become visible, along with its connection to all of life. No wonder we expect the worst.

But our wisdom isn't the wisdom of Genesis. In the end this isn't a story of judgment but a story of grace. The story is heavy with pain as it speaks the truth. But the truth is spoken as graciously here as in the rest of the Bible. This is the story of God accepting Adam and Eve just the way they are. God respects the choice they've made, even though God may have hoped for a different outcome.

This is also the story of God seeing Adam and Eve through grace-filled eyes. God doesn't treat Adam and Eve as though they were mistakes or must now be humiliated. The story of Adam and Eve leaves no doubt that God holds both Adam and Eve responsible for their actions. God doesn't look the other way. There are painful, back-breaking consequences as well as death ahead for each of them. Yet God meets their need without shaming or destroying them.

God clothes Adam and Eve. God makes for them what they couldn't make for themselves. God covers what they couldn't hide. God gives Adam and Eve the gift of seeing each other again—not as enemies but as needy partners in the hard life that lies ahead. God covers them with grace and invites them to see each other as human beings covered with grace. God doesn't abandon Adam and Eve but is present with them in the conception and birth of their first child.

We've become accustomed to holding up Adam and Eve as bad examples. Whatever they did, we're not to repeat their error. Or if we want to avoid their error, we're told it's impossible. Their sin was so powerful that the error of their way is the error of our way. We've learned to hear the Bible holding up Adam and Eve as the prime example of how *not* to relate to God or to each other. Then we announce gloomily in the same breath that it's too late to do anything about it anyway. No wonder the story comes across as bad news. Not just about who we are, but about what we can expect from the rest of the Bible.

We believe the story of Adam and Eve proclaims the same good news that's proclaimed everywhere in the Bible. God accepts each of us just as we are—with our good human limitations, and in our fallen condition. Because it's the bearer of good news the Bible is already our friend, not our enemy. It is a *good* book. A means of grace, not a means of harsh judgment. It invites us to hear God's acceptance of Adam and Eve as God's acceptance of *us*. Beyond that, it invites us into a new way of listening to its pages. Listening as a friend.

PART II:
A Process for Making Friends with the Bible

Introduction

I used to feel guilty about how I treated the Bible. Reading the Bible was like praying. I never did enough of either. I was always afraid people would ask me how much of the Bible I had read. Worse yet, they might ask how much time I spent each day reading it. When they finally got around to asking, my worst fears were usually confirmed. I was a failure. The only thing I thought I could do about it was try harder.

But making friends with the Bible doesn't have to do with how often I read it or how many chapters and books I've read in it. A friend once asked me how many times I had read the Bible from beginning to end. I started counting with a college class in which I was required to do this. Then I went on to name the many times since then when I had tried but never finished. When my friend informed me she was starting on her twelfth time through the Bible, I was shocked. Maybe I wasn't taking the Bible seriously.

Making friends with the Bible has to do with *how* I read

it, not with how many *times* I read it. One of my college professors used to put a series of letters on the chalkboard: G O D I S N O W H E R E. The important thing was *how* I read these letters, not how many *times* I read them. If I hide from the Bible as I read it, I'll never know it as a friend. It won't matter how often or how much I've read.

The Bible asks the same question every time I open it. What will I do with this witness? Will I give it freedom to speak, or will I silence it? I silence the Bible every time I hide from it. I bind it, instead of setting it free to give me its good news.

We don't have a formula for making friends with the Bible or a set of rules that guarantee success. Instead, we have a process. We developed it by thinking about our own experience of making friends with the Bible. The process has seven steps which invite you to focus on specific attitudes and activities. We've found they help us free the Bible to be a witness to God's good news. We invite you to try them for yourselves. Along with the steps, we've included exercises and checklists to help you put them into practice.

Before describing the steps, we want to describe what you can expect as you go through this process. Unrealistic expectations can spell disaster before friendship has a chance to grow between two people. In the same way, unrealistic expectations will hinder you from the very beginning as you attempt to befriend the Bible. These expectations have also been drawn from our own experience. In some ways they are even more important than the steps themselves.

1. Expect this process to take time and energy.

Recently a young woman I've known for several years came into my office. Her look of contentment took me by surprise. I knew she had gone through several confusing and painful experiences during the last six months. During that time she had married someone she later discovered was an active alcoholic. Her mother had died of a burst appendix, the result of poor medical attention, and she had begun a lawsuit against the doctor. She and her new husband had moved into her alcoholic father's home to help him deal with his loss, only to discover that Dad was suffering from Alzheimer's disease. Her thirty-five year old brother also lived in the house, which he used as a center for his drug parties. In the last few weeks she had been experiencing panic attacks that kept her from going out, even to the grocery store.

But today she looked peaceful. When I asked about this, she told me she had just found a new book about how relationships work, was reading all about it, and was sure that everything would now be all right!

Friendship with the Bible won't happen just because you're reading this book. Making friends with the Bible is a process, not an event. It won't happen unless you invest significant time and energy, taking active responsibility for your own relationship to the Bible. Even when you invest time and energy, things won't happen overnight. Nor will they happen once for all. Significant friendships take sustained attention. So does friendship with the Bible.

2. Expect progress, not perfection.

This process doesn't have a grand finale. Over time, however, you will be able to describe a "before" and an "after" in your friendship with the Bible. This doesn't mean all parts of "after" will feel equally comfortable or reassuring. It doesn't mean you'll never again feel stuck or discouraged. Rather, it means you'll know you're moving. Sometimes this may feel like going backwards.

Progress doesn't mean you're becoming a Bible expert. It means you're learning to stop hiding from the

Bible. It means you don't feel as much need to control what it says or who needs to hear what it says right now. It means you're learning to let the biblical witness speak for itself. And it means you're learning from your mistakes as you go along.

3. Expect change.

This process will invite and challenge you to change. This may include not just your understanding of what the Bible means, but your attitudes and behaviors toward the Bible. It may include some of your comfortable beliefs about yourself, about God, about other people in your life, or about how things work in this world. It may include looking into some unfinished business from your past.

The invitation to change may come at any point in the process. Though you may find some steps easier than others, there isn't any one step or exercise that's necessarily more likely to challenge you than others. We invite you to keep an open mind as you work through each step. Change is always painful and difficult. It means letting go of some things that have become comfortable, even though they may be hurting us or others. But change can also be invigorating. One thing is certain. Only *you* will know whether you're ready to change, and how much.

4. Expect your relationship to the Bible to look different than anyone else's.

We have a habit of expecting everyone's way of relating to the Bible to look the same. Usually this means we expect it to look like some idealized picture we carry around in our minds. This is strange, since we don't usually have trouble acknowledging that two different people may relate to a third person in very different ways. In fact, we become suspicious if too many people begin relating to the same person in the same way. We wonder what's going on, and whether this central figure is either controlling or being controlled by everyone else. We've heard horror stories about people like Jim Jones and the members of his People's Temple, all of whom ended up following the leader to mass suicide.

Like any friend, the Bible is capable of being responded to in many ways. Because of our limited sight, we don't know what our new friendship with the Bible is going to look like or how other people will respond when they see it. This means friendship with the Bible can feel lonely. Not everyone will be happy to see me come out of my hiding places and begin making friends with the Bible, especially if I don't follow their ideas about how people should relate to the Bible.

Differences between people always become more visible when silence is broken. Making friends with the Bible means breaking your silence about what you think the Bible says. It means admitting how you feel today about what you're reading and hearing, and which parts you find disturbing or puzzling. Most of us are uncomfortable when differences become visible. But they can be a sign that we're beginning to take responsibility for our own relationships to the Bible. No one can make friends with the Bible for you or for me. We can only describe for ourself how the Bible connects with our sometimes very different worlds.

5. Expect surprises.

Change is difficult. Most of us avoid it even when we know we need it. We fear the unknown, and we fear what might happen on the way from here to there. This process invites you to be open to change. But it also invites you to expect surprises along the way. Good surprises. They will happen when you least expect them. You can't manufacture or plan for them. But you can expect them as you work on this process.

The Bible itself may surprise you. It may not be as dull, harshly judgmental, naive, and outdated as you fear.

You may surprise yourself. Perhaps you'll have more insights into the meaning of the Bible than you think you will.

Other people may surprise you with their insights into the Bible. They may not be as dull or judgmental or unlike you as you may expect them to be.

Finally, God may surprise you. You may begin to discover God's presence in unexpected places. Not just in the Bible, but in life itself.

Step One

Focus first on myself,
not on the Bible

I love to fish. And I love to watch people fishing. Some of them keep detailed log books in which they record stages of the moon, water temperature, weather conditions, which way the wind is blowing, and anything else that might signal good fishing times. My grandfather was like this. He never went fishing if a south wind was blowing. Then there are the rest of us. We just pick up our poles when we have time, head for the spot where we last saw fish, and leave the rest to luck!

Most of us approach Bible study the way we approach fishing. We don't have time to approach it as though it were a science. So we just open the Bible and hope we'll get lucky.

Step One in this process doesn't invite you to keep a log book, but it does invite you to notice what's going on in your life. How are you feeling today? What did you spend most of your time thinking about yesterday or last night? What were you doing in the hours or minutes just before you sat down to read the Bible?

Step One asks you to take a quick inventory of what your life looks like today. It doesn't ask you to make judgments about what your life *should* look like. It just asks you to state what it *does* look like. The point isn't to identify what needs to be fixed up, so that you become eligible to open the Bible. The point is to become visible to yourself.

If hiding from the Bible means turning attention away from myself, then the first step in making friends with the Bible is to focus on myself. This means making a conscious choice *not* to focus first on the Bible itself, or on what we think it means. It means deciding to spend quiet time clarifying what I bring today to this encounter with the Bible.

Sometimes I volunteer to cover for the chaplain in our community hospital. I'm required to write a summary of each visit for the chaplain to review. The very first question on the summary form has nothing to do with the situation I'm about to encounter. It's about me. "What was your state of mind, and what was going on in your life just before you made this pastoral visit?" I have a history. I didn't just materialize on this planet. My history affects whatever I set out to do, whether I'm aware of it or not.

Focusing on my present situation lets me hear the noise and confusion, identify it, and perhaps reduce it. It helps me become aware of things that will affect the way I listen to the Bible today. Most important, it makes visible the connection between my world and the world of the Bible. In fact, my present situation *is* my connection to the Bible. I don't have to look beyond my own life for other connections. The connection exists even before I open the pages of the Bible.

This is a small step. In friendship, little things mean a lot. The rest of the world may never see them. But if they could be gathered together, these little things would reveal the truth about the nature of our friendships. The same is true about our friendship with the Bible. When we talk about coming out of hiding from the Bible, it may seem we're talking about a great exposé, or a moment of truth that will be announced with trumpets and fanfare. But this isn't what we mean.

When we come out of hiding from the Bible, there's a sense in which nothing changes. From the outside everything may look the same as ever. We still relate to the Bible by reading and studying it, sometimes in church or in Bible study, sometimes on our own. But there's one small step that makes all the difference. We begin by turning the focus on ourselves, not on the Bible or on what it says about me or about other people.

Resistance to this seemingly small change is phenomenal. We do *not* like to focus on ourselves. In fact, we may be convinced there are good reasons why we shouldn't.

Many people believe it just isn't very spiritual to focus on ourselves instead of the Bible. In fact, some would say it's self-centered and probably comes from thinking more highly of ourselves than we ought to. It might even mean we have a low view of the Bible. Isn't it much more important to investigate the Bible than to spend time looking at ourselves? Surely the *Bible's* thoughts and words are more trustworthy than our own.

As sincere as this objection is, it misses the point of coming out of hiding. The point isn't to set the Bible aside and enthrone ourselves. Rather, the point is to begin looking at the way we relate to the Bible. If I want to befriend the Bible, I can't treat it as though *it* were the only object of investigation. I must also investigate myself. I must be as honest and clear as I can about what *I* am bringing to the relationship today.

Some people raise another objection. Turning attention to ourselves means ignoring what we see as problems in the Bible. We should begin by being honest and clear about such problems. We wouldn't want anyone, including ourselves, to be misled because of them. Some problems are serious, and it's only honest for us to admit this and then do what we can to resolve the concerns and promote a more informed view of the Bible.

Entire books have been devoted to taking seriously parts of the Bible that seem inconsistent. Sometimes this is done by changing the meanings of texts to prove that the Bible has no conflicting information. Other times it's done by questioning the reliability of one text to deal with potentially embarrassing differences in another text. In both cases, the present-day author's own viewpoint has been taken more seriously than the Bible's.

We *do* need to take everything about the Bible seriously. But this objection may say more about us than about the Bible. It may say we think the Bible doesn't meet *our* standards, which are presumably higher than the Bible's. It assumes we're supposed to keep people from misusing and misunderstanding this book, though not even God is safe from misuse and misunderstanding. Such a view overlooks the way God has worked in this world ever since Adam and Eve. God has always worked through things this world considers problematic, weak, and insignificant.

If we want to make friends with the Bible, taking it seriously doesn't mean keeping track of its problems and trying to resolve them. Friendship with other people doesn't work very well this way. Neither does friendship with the Bible. Clarity about myself is the key to clarity about my friends. Have I taken seriously what *I* am bringing to friendship with the Bible?

Finally, some people believe that if we focus first on ourselves we'll miss addressing the needs of people around us. As friends of the Bible, is it not our privilege and our duty to point out how much the Bible has to offer to these people? And isn't it important, then, to begin with an analysis of their situation and their needs? Haven't I focused too narrowly and even individualistically when I begin with myself? Perhaps I'll end up just talking to and about myself.

This objection is understandable, but it also misses the point. The Bible does indeed proclaim good news for the entire human family. However, the point is that the people around me don't need to hear what I think the Bible is saying to them or to their situation. Instead, they need to hear my witness to what I'm discovering in this book about *my* situation.

How my witness connects with other people is important, but it isn't my first concern. My first concern is what I am bringing to my encounter with the Bible, not what others are bringing. In fact, the more I think about what others need to hear from the Bible, the more likely I am to read my own voice into the text. This is rarely good news for other people in my life!

When I was growing up, one of my favorite times in church was also one of my least favorite. I loved to hear other church members stand up and give what we called "personal testimonies." I loved hearing regular people talk about how the Bible was speaking to them in their journeys with God. Unfortunately, some of them used this time to talk about what they thought the Bible was saying to them about *me*, or about all of us together. My heart turned and ran from these experiences. I would gladly have hidden under a pew if I could have done so without drawing attention to myself.

Many of us approach Bible study with the idea that we're supposed to find in it something other people need to hear. Step One invites you to try another approach. The exercise that follows will help you get started.

Working it out

1. Get some paper and a pencil. You might want to use a notebook or journal.

2. Identify your situation right now. Ask yourself a few questions. How am I feeling today? Am I in conflict over someone or something? Am I content, happy, grieving? What has happened in the last forty-eight hours of my life? What feelings have I experienced during that period? What circumstances gave rise to these feelings? Write it down. (Remember, this is a quick inventory, not an autobiography!)

3. Choose any passage from the Bible that seems to form a unit—a story, a parable, a lesson, a psalm. It should be longer than one verse, but not too long to read in several minutes.

4. If you've chosen a familiar text, take a few minutes to jot down the way you've usually heard this text interpreted.

5. Now read the text from beginning to end. Make a list of words, phrases, subjects, themes, or other things that stand out to you.

6. Compare this list with what you wrote in response to item 2, and answer this question. Is there any connection between things that are going on in my life and things I see in this text? Name the connections.

7. If you don't see any connection yet, don't be discouraged. You may need to live with this text for a while. You may want to give yourself time to think over not just what's in the text, but what's going on in your life right now. When you've gotten in touch with yourself, you'll begin to see connections. Write them down.

8. Finally, what are your worst fears about this text? What are you afraid it means? What are you afraid it might mean for *you? Write it down.*

What this looks like

The following example will give you an idea of what this step looks like. It is taken from Elouise's personal notebook. I've reproduced only some of my notes word for word, since they contain private material. However, you will still be able to see what happens when you begin by focusing on yourself. I've also included a few explanatory notes along the way.

1. I use a notebook, and date my entries. Sometimes I work on a text for several days or even weeks. It's helpful and encouraging to look back and see how I've progressed, not just in my understanding of the text, but of what's going on in my life.

2. It took about ten minutes to do this item. Following is a summary of material in my notebook.

I woke up today with a lot of anxiety. I can feel it in my gut. I have fears about my daughter going away next week to school in New York. New York is a tough city. I don't yet know how we'll work out all the finances for her housing. I'm going through difficult changes in some close relationships, and am anxious about how it will all work out. I've been working on a writing project all summer. It isn't finished yet, and classes begin in a few weeks. I'm not ready. It's rainy and gray outside.

3. I chose Psalm 23. When I began, I had no idea what passage I would look at. Usually that's already decided for me. This time Psalm 23 suggested itself to me the moment I came to the end of the second item, above. It felt right, though I wasn't sure why.

4. Usually I hear Psalm 23 read or quoted at funerals as a source of comfort. I don't usually hear it preached from or studied in a systematic way. When I do, I often hear a description of how dumb sheep are (and human beings, too). The funeral context suggests a generally understood

interpretation: God is taking care of us and won't abandon us, even when things are at their bleakest.

    5. Here's what jumped off the page at me, in this order:
        —the darkest valley (v. 4)
        —enemies (v. 5)
        —my whole life long (v. 6)
        —no fear of evil (v. 4)
        —God's presence (a theme throughout)
        —all needs met (a theme throughout)

    6. Following is exactly what I wrote in my notebook regarding connections between the list in item 5 and what I wrote in response to item 2.

    The connections seem obvious. I don't feel like the person singing this psalm. I feel like an abandoned sheep—left alone without a shepherd. I'm in a dark valley. It's rainy and gray outside, which matches what's going on inside. I'm afraid New York is full of enemies who will get my daughter. My head knows God is present, but my gut hasn't gotten the message. I feel incredibly needy today. The connection to this psalm is negative. I am not the sheep of this psalm. Whoever wrote this wasn't having a bad day.

    7. The connection was made, though I was surprised at how much my daughter's move to New York was weighing me down. I knew my main problem wasn't fear of New York itself. It was grief over her leaving. She must begin making her way in this world as a woman, just as I have and must continue to do. On that particular day, I didn't feel I was making my way very well, so my fears for her had escalated.

    8. My worst fear is that this psalm won't work unless I'm having a good day. I'm afraid it will mean nothing for me today. I'm afraid I'll spend time on this text, and nothing will change. I'll still feel as anxious and fearful at the end of this process as I do right now.

Step Two

Accept my limitations as good

I remember a student of mine who struggled to keep up with his classmates. He couldn't read well because of several learning disabilities. So he spent long hours each day and night on homework that most of my students could finish in thirty minutes. He wanted to be a lawyer. His parents, with every good intention, told him he could be whatever he wanted. Even though he drove himself constantly, in the end he usually understood little of what he studied. Neither he nor his parents understood that true achievement begins with accepting limitations.

When I come out of hiding from the Bible, the first thing it shows me is the last thing I want to accept. I may be prepared for it to show me how sinful and wretched I am. But the Bible doesn't begin with my sin. It begins with the goodness of human limitations.

Adam and Eve didn't want to live within their limitations. Neither do we. We want to see as God sees. But we can't even get started looking in the right direction. God sees our limitations and pronounces them good. We look at the same limitations and pronounce them bad!

We're especially blind to human limitations every time we fall in love. We're all romantics at heart. We want a friend who will always be there for us, never disappoint us, and never say no. We want someone who can read our minds and our hearts, anticipate every response, and always say just the right thing. At the same time, we know the frustration of dealing with so-called friends who think they know us better than we know ourselves. Sometimes they feel entitled to make decisions for us. Often they can't take no for an answer.

True friendship begins with accepting limitations. So does friendship with the Bible. As you work through the process of making friends with the Bible, you will encounter several limitations over and over again. They aren't embarrassing obstacles, or weaknesses you need to overcome. They are good. They are, in fact, part of the process. This step invites you not only to acknowledge these limitations but also to accept them as good.

The first limitations you'll encounter are your limited time and resources. Face it. Once you begin studying the Bible, you'll never think you have enough time. And once you begin seeing how many things you'd like to know more about, you'll never think you have enough resources.

So right at the beginning, this step invites you to be realistic. It's easy to name what we *wish* we could do. It's much more difficult to name what we might realistically do, given our present circumstances and other responsibilities.

How much time can I *realistically* expect to spend on this text? And what resources are realistically available to me today? You may have very little time. You may have few resources. You may feel embarrassed, discouraged, or even apologetic about this. You may be tempted to look at these limitations and pronounce them bad.

But this step is about accepting limitations as good. Making friends with the Bible isn't about going to heroic or extraordinary measures to prove you take the Bible seriously. Neither is it a competitive sport. Rather, it's about becoming content with what you have. It's about becoming a good steward of whatever time and resources you've been given today. It's about discovering in your seemingly little time and few resources *more* than enough to satisfy your hunger.

Making friends with the Bible means making peace with our limited time and resources. It also means making peace with our limited understanding.

Two elderly women lived on the same mountain. One day they met in a village not far from the mountain. As they talked about their homes, they got into an argument about the mountain. One insisted it was rocky and barren. The other protested vehemently that it was green, with soft rolling hills. Each accused the other of being blind.

In fact, one of them lived on the east side facing land, and the other on the west side facing the ocean. Neither had traveled to the other side of the mountain. But each thought she knew exactly what the mountain was like.

Our understanding of the Bible is limited by our experience of the world and of life. We've each seen a corner, but none of us has seen it all. Our experiences are invaluable resources in our study of the Bible. But they do not set the limits for what the Bible may or may not mean.

People who don't see it the way I see it aren't necessarily blind. They may never have seen what I have seen, just as I've never seen what they have seen. Their understanding of the Bible is as limited by their experience of the world and of life as is mine. Perhaps we could sit down and talk to each other.

Ever since Adam and Eve, we've denied the goodness of our limited understanding, especially when it comes to reading the Bible. We may proclaim loudly that we have limited understanding, but our actions betray us. Before we open the Bible we often ask God to illuminate our minds as we read, so that we'll see all things clearly. We pray for new eyes, eyes not clouded by the limitations of this world. We don't realize we've just asked God to give us what the serpent offered Adam and Eve!

Sometimes we don't stop to ask God for this. We just assume or hope that when we read the Bible, our limited understanding will somehow be set aside. The power of the Bible itself will do this. But the Bible will never give us eyes to see just as God sees, not even when we're reading the Bible itself. It will never cancel the effects of our limited understanding.

Our actions also betray us when we gather for group Bible study. Perhaps someone has an insight we think we should have had first. Or someone points out a flaw in our interpretation, or a side of the problem they think we should have seen. Our embarrassment, and even our guilty feelings about being caught in our limitations, betrays our desire to see as God sees.

This step isn't about being embarrassed or ashamed because of limitations. It's about learning to accept them as a productive part of the process. I will understand today what I am ready to understand. That is all I need to understand right now. I can relax; God doesn't expect me to go any further today than my limitations allow.

Knowing I'm ready for whatever I see in the Bible today can make me eager to move ahead. Opening the Bible is a little like peeking through the door on Christmas morning to see what gifts are waiting under the tree. In fact, it's even better. I *know* the gift I receive from the Bible will be just right.

Accepting limitations doesn't mean understanding has come to a dead end. The opposite is true. It means I've decided to keep my mind open for further discoveries. I don't completely understand any part of the Bible. I've seen a corner, but I haven't seen it all.

The goodness of our limited understanding often becomes visible in group Bible study. Each interprets the Bible from a different, limited perspective. No one sees the Bible fully and completely. But sometimes when we share our limited understandings, we see something in the Bible that none of us would have seen alone.

Last week I led a Bible study on Luke's story of the good Samaritan. People in the group began going on and on about how different things are today. No one would stop to help you today, even if you were lying half-dead on the side of the highway.

A woman in the group said quietly but with great conviction, "That's not true."

The group didn't know that four years earlier this woman had been beaten, raped, stabbed thirty times, and left for dead. She survived because strangers came to her aid.

Her connection with the text helped all of us find our connection to the text. Luke wasn't inviting us to criticize the present age. He was inviting us to go and do likewise. To be the stranger with eyes to see, who takes time to do what needs to be done. Or to allow such a stranger to come to *our* aid.

Step Two invites you to accept your limited time, resources, and understanding, so you can get on with using what you've been given. It isn't an invitation to laziness or an excuse for not seeking to broaden your present understanding. Rather, it's an encouragement to do what you can, given your limitations. This is all God asks of us.

Working it out

1. Estimate and write down the approximate amount of time you have to spend on this passage today or this week.

2. Record the present time of day.

3. Reread the passage you've chosen and make a list of anything you *don't* understand—words, images, ideas, the way people treat each other in the story, teachings that seem vague or complicated. Anything.

4. What resources do you have that may be useful as you work on this passage? List any that are readily and realistically available to you. Include anything that might help you understand this text—teachers, pastors, friends, commentaries, other books.

5. Using the list you've just made, put a check mark beside the resources you would like to consult (given the amount of time you have for this study). Then make a list of those you've checked, putting resources you think will be most helpful at the top of the list.

6. Keep going. Don't be discouraged if you have little time or resources. The point isn't to become a Bible scholar, but to remind yourself of your limitations.

7. What time is it?

What this looks like

(Psalm 23, continued from previous chapter)

1. I decided to spend about one hour on this text, and to begin right after lunch. My notes indicate I was feeling low and didn't want to turn this into a major project. There were other things I wanted to do that day. I stopped first to eat lunch, because skipping lunch only contributes to my problems.

2. I began this part of the exercise at 2:00 p.m.

3. The main thing I didn't understand on that particular

day was how *anyone* could walk through the darkest valley and *fear no evil* (v. 4). It took about ten minutes to come to this realization.

4. Given my limited time, I identified only several resources, all available in my house.

> —King James Version of Psalm 23 (which I memorized as a child)
> —commentaries on the Psalms (several at home)
> —Oxford Annotated Bible (RSV with notes)
> —Leland Ryken, *How to Read the Bible as Literature* (has a brief discussion of the psalm as a literary form)

5. Given my time limit, I listed only two of these resources: Ryken's book, and the Oxford Annotated Bible. I already had the King James version in memory.

6. Because I've studied the Bible in academic settings, and am a Bible scholar, I felt uncomfortable leaving commentaries off my list of most helpful resources. However, letting go of any need to check out commentaries was part of accepting my limitations on that day. Though I find commentaries useful in working on the text, I don't rely heavily on them when I'm just beginning my work. So not consulting them at all simply underscored the intent of this part of the process, which is to gain clarity about what *I* think the text might mean.

7. I finished this exercise at about 2:15 p.m. I had used fifteen minutes of my hour.

Step Three

Accept the Bible just as it is

One hot dry day in August, a farmer stood looking out over his field to a friend's neighboring farm. His good friend's eldest daughter was pulling a heavily loaded hay wagon across the rough terrain. His casual attention turned to alarm as he saw the wagon topple and land upside down on the pile of hay. He ran across the field and found the young woman unharmed but understandably distressed.

"Why don't you just leave this here for now?" he asked. "Come over to our house and get some lunch. We'll clean this up later."

"Oh no," she replied. "I don't think my father would like that."

"Nonsense!" he insisted. "Your father and I have shared many a meal in times of trouble."

She began to protest again, but he would hear no more of her objections. So they went back to his house for lunch.

After a leisurely lunch they returned to the wagon.

"Don't you feel better, now that you've eaten?" he asked.

"Yes," she responded. "But I'm still sure my father isn't going to be pleased."

"Don't be so sure," he said. "I know your father isn't that hard to get along with. By the way, where is your father today?"

"That's what I was trying to tell you," the young woman exclaimed. "He's under the hay wagon!"

Even with the best of intentions, we sometimes don't pay attention to the Bible. We overlook or ignore what the Bible is trying to tell us about itself. We don't always accept the Bible just as it is.

Sometimes this means we deny its humanity. Even though the Bible addresses all of life in one way or another, it doesn't present itself as a full and complete book about everything. But instead of accepting its limitations as good, we take the Bible as though it claimed to be a full and complete account, especially when we want it to be on our side or tell us what to do.

We try to escape our own limited and distorted understanding by appealing to the Bible as though it could fill in the gaps, making our understanding full and complete. But it can't. This doesn't mean the Bible has a problem. It means *we* have a problem. Perhaps we don't want to accept ourselves just as we are. But we may also fear accepting the Bible just as it is. It might lose its power if we accept its humanity.

Part of the Bible's humanity is the humanity of the people who wrote parts of it down or decided what would be included in its pages. The Bible presents itself as the witness of human beings who are like we are, even though they live in different times and places. Like us, they have human limitations and live in a fallen world. Like us, they are learning to come out of hiding and trust God instead of their fears. To overlook the Bible's humanity is also to overlook their humanity.

We believe the Bible's witnesses are reliable and inspired. This doesn't mean, however, that they were protected from their human limitations and the distortions of their fallenness. Inspiration doesn't mean God removes human limitations and fallenness. The apostle Paul confesses his human limitations and his sin at the same time that he offers his words for God to use in the Christian churches of his day. We can rely on this: Paul and all the others were human beings living in a fallen world.

Perhaps you won't find this very reassuring. It may seem this leaves no room for the Bible to be anything more than the words of limited and fallen human beings. But this would be failure to count on God. Paul argues that his words should be heard not because of him, but because of God. He knows God works through the weak things of this world.

The Bible is the written Word of God not because of the work of its human authors and editors, but because of the work of God. This doesn't mean God ignores, violates, or scorns the effort of these individuals. On the contrary, God honors their work, with all its human limitations and fallenness. The words in the Bible are the words of human beings witnessing faithfully to what they have seen and heard. Our own histories demonstrate that God has chosen to accept their offering, to use their combined witness as a chief means of grace in this fallen world. The written Word of God is inspired because God breathes life into its pages, today as well as yesterday.

Sometimes refusal to accept the Bible just as it is means we deny its unique status as the written Word of God. The Bible also presents itself in *this* way, not because it knows this about itself in advance, but because over the centuries this identity has become visible in the way God has used it.

This doesn't mean the Bible has led an enchanted life or that its identity has been clear to everyone who comes in contact with it. God isn't the only one who has used this book over the centuries. There have always been people who have misused the Bible, or found it quaint and even laughable. Yet God's persistence in using the Bible just as it is has become an intrinsic part of its identity. God refuses to relegate it to oblivion, in spite of the way we human beings have misused and mistreated it.

It's painful to confess that the Bible, just as it is, may be the written Word of God, especially when we think we've been called to save it. We sometimes try to escape the embarrassment of being seen with it by making ourselves the judges of the Bible.

When I was in elementary school I was sometimes embarrassed to be seen with less popular classmates. I was afraid everyone would think I was as immature, obnoxious, or mean as they seemed to be. I was afraid I would be shunned as these classmates were. I always felt better when my teachers and other classmates assigned me the role of protector, in charge of fixing up the unpopular ones. That made it clear that I was better than they were.

Some of us like to play the same role in relation to the Bible. Instead of denying the humanity of its authors and editors, we affirm it loudly—though regretfully. We then hold up our own enlightened humanity as a better standard for what should or shouldn't be in this text. We think ourselves more observant, more compassionate, more informed, more loving, and even more inspired than the biblical authors were.

The Bible has a twofold identity which many of us find difficult to accept. It is written by humans, and it comes from God in a unique way. It's easy to focus on one side or the other. Some of us fear accepting the Bible's humanity, since this seems to take away from its status as the inspired

Word of God. It seems to make it just one book among many. Others fear accepting this book as uniquely from God. This seems to ignore the Bible's roots in human times, human places, and human situations.

Both fears are valid. However, we believe that accepting these two sides of the Bible's identity *together* is the best way to address both fears. The Bible's twofold identity is good news. Anything less waters down the witness.

It's good news that the authors and editors of the Bible were limited, fallen humans who lived in a fallen world. Their words are not the witness of pure, holy, righteous people living in splendid isolation and security above it all. They are the words of people just like we are. People who lived with joy, sorrow, and moral dilemmas just as we do. People who struggled with relationships just as we do. People who had to live one day at a time just as we do. We don't have to strain to make connections with the biblical world. The connections are already there, waiting for us to discover them.

It's good news that there is diversity *and* difference in the Bible. The voices of these witnesses weren't absorbed into one chosen spokesperson's voice. God's truth is greater than any one witness. The many pages of the Bible and the complexity of its witness give us hope. Here is concrete evidence that God's truth is proclaimed in and through the many times, places, and forms of our limited and fallen humanity. God conveys grace through this book not in spite of but by *means* of diversity and difference within its own strange chorus of witnesses.

It's good news that the Bible is God's written Word. Even though I am invited to connect with its pages, the work of this book in my life does not depend on my grasp of all its words. Nor does it depend on anyone else's grasp of its words. There is more going on than any of us sees. The Bible is part of the mystery of God's ways with humanity. As we become friends with the Bible, these words will work in our lives in ways we cannot control and may never fully understand. Just as God acted centuries ago to bring to birth the witness given in these pages, so God acts through these pages today to bring new life to birth.

Taking seriously both sides of the Bible's identity means attending carefully to the details of the text just as it presents itself to us. This isn't always easy or comfortable.

Recently I led a Bible study on Luke. In Luke 10:25 a lawyer asks Jesus what he must do to inherit eternal life. Jesus answers that he must love God with all his heart, soul, strength, and mind, and his neighbor as himself. Then in Luke 18:18 a ruler asks Jesus the same question. This time Jesus says the ruler must sell all he owns, distribute the money to the poor, and follow Jesus.

People in the Bible study were comfortable with Jesus' answer to the first man. But they wanted immediately to soften the blow of his answer to the second man by referring to other verses in the Bible.

If we take seriously both sides of the Bible's identity, we will attend to every nuance of the text, without explaining away or softening what we find difficult or disturbing. We'll listen not just to the words themselves, but to the attitudes and emotions being conveyed through these carefully chosen words. We'll think about the order in which the various parts of the text have been skillfully and artfully arranged. We'll look for the text's own clues about the situations of writers and of the people for whom these words were recorded.

This doesn't mean we will understand or even see all the details of the text. We won't. We'll see what we are ready to see. We may never understand all the details we notice. But careful attention to them demonstrates acceptance of the Bible just as it is. It indicates we're open to whatever God may want to accomplish in our lives through this book.

Working it out

1. (Note the time whenever you begin or stop working on your passage.) Look again at the passage you've chosen. *Without consulting any outside resources,* answer some of the following questions.

a. Do *two or three details* stand out to you in this text? Write them down. They may include specific words, phrases, patterns of repetition, parallels and contrasts, descriptive words and phrases, who speaks and who listens, who takes initiative and who responds, themes, images, attitudes, emotions.

You might try reading the text out loud to highlight details you may miss when you read it silently.

How do these details help you understand what's going on in this text? (Let the text itself help you understand the details. Don't reach yet for outside resources.)

b. Can you identify *the form of the text*? If it's a story, what kind of story does it seem to be? Is it a sermon? A lesson? A psalm? A poem? A proverb? A prophecy? A letter? A vision? A genealogy? A set of laws or instructions?

Why do you think this text is in this form? Does the form give you any clues about the meaning of the text itself, or the effect it might have on you and other readers?

c. Who is named as *the writer of the text*? This is an important detail, even though you may not agree that the person named actually wrote the text. Perhaps you know nothing about this person except what is stated at the beginning of the particular book from which you are reading. How does even that bit of information help you understand the text you're studying? Do you see any connections?

d. What *human time, place, or situation* does this text

seem to have in mind? Does the text tell you directly? If so, what do you learn from the text itself? If the text doesn't tell you directly, what conclusions can you draw based on clues in the text? How does any of this help you understand the text better?

e. What *connection* do you see with whatever comes right before and right after this text? Why do you think this text comes where it does? How does this help you understand what's going on in the text itself?

f. Do you see any connection between this passage and *other passages in the Bible*? If so, what are they? How does this help you better understand the text?

2. Now go back to Step Two, to the list of things you don't understand in this text. Is there anything you want to add to your list or remove from it? How are you doing? Is the text making more sense? What would you like to pursue further?

Look at your list of resources. Using whatever you think will be most helpful, use your resources to pursue further anything you don't yet understand. As you work, jot down insights or data you find helpful.

3. Now read the text again. Is there something you wish the text said differently? Why does it bother you? How would *you* say it, in contrast to the way you think the text says it? Write it down.

4. Given your present understanding, can you name some things you're pretty sure this text doesn't mean, or isn't about? Next name what you think it does mean, or is about.

5. How is this text the story of your life? Can you identify yourself in any of the characters? In each of them? Is your situation like the writer's? Like the situation of the intended audience or readers? How does this text connect with your life right now? Write it down.

What this looks like

(Psalm 23, continued from previous chapter)

1. *It's now 2:15 p.m. I've chosen to work on details in the text, and on the form of the text.*

a. Here are details that stood out to me on that particular day.

—Verse 6 says "whole life long" instead of "forever" (the way I memorized it). This means the last verse isn't just about living with God someday in heaven. It's about living my whole life long with God—right now.

—The psalm pictures God leading me, and ends with goodness and mercy following me. God goes before me, is with me, and follows me. This means I am surrounded in time by God's presence.

—Verses 4 and 5 describe hard things, which is where I feel I am today, even though I can imagine worse.

—The one thing that doesn't change no matter what's being described in the psalm is God's presence. God is dependable, in *every* changing situation.

b. The *form* of the text is a psalm. It has David's name in the heading, and sounds like a personal statement. This isn't an essay about doctrine. It's a song of faith in God who is my shepherd. The psalm invites me to identify with the feelings and experiences of a sheep who has the best shepherd it could possibly have.

Because it's a song it expresses deep feeling. It isn't trying to teach me something. It's inviting me to feel something. I think it's inviting me to feel things like trust, gratitude, rest and comfort, peace. Not because everything is rosy, but because someone more powerful than I is leading me.

The places I'm being taken in my life aren't accidental. They are part of a journey God has prepared for *me*. God goes with me and follows behind me in this journey.

2. Going back to Step Two, I didn't understand how anyone could be in the darkest valley and fear no evil. Here's what I wrote in my notebook.

I think there isn't any head logic to this that's persuasive. The only way to understand, I think, is to be there. Then the words make sense. It's also clear that God is present even though I haven't come necessarily to the darkest valley of my life—"objectively speaking." I'm beginning to understand that this is about a history the psalmist (David?) has already had with God. It isn't about an isolated day in the life of the psalmist. It's about the psalmist's "whole life long."

Deciding I wanted to know more about psalms, I looked at pages 114-118 in Ryken's *How to Read the Bible as Literature*, and my notes indicate the following.

Ryken puts Psalm 23 in the category of praise psalms, and makes the point that these psalms direct attention to God, not to the psalmist. This is so, even though these psalms describe the speaker's feelings. This confirms details noted above. Also it helps answer my question. The psalmist can fear no evil because attention is being directed to *God*, not to the darkest valley itself, as though the *valley* were the main thing. At the same time, *only being in the valley* leads to this kind of praise to God.

3. On that day I found nothing I wished the text said differently.

4. Here's what I thought this text meant and didn't mean, given my understanding at that time.

—It doesn't mean life with God as my shepherd will be easy, or that with God as my shepherd I don't have to do anything because God will magically make it all work out.

—It isn't just for funerals, though it clearly is for hard times.

—It isn't about some disconnected state of tranquillity, above it all.

—It is about God's presence throughout my whole life long, going before me to prepare what I need, and following after me with goodness and mercy.

—It's about real life with God. I'm reminded of Adam and Eve! This could have been their song. Before and after the Fall.

5. This text invites me to see there's more going on in my life than I'm feeling today. It invites me to remember the places God has led me in the past in order to get to this day. In fact, there are good reasons for my discomfort, fear, and anxiety today. I'm going through some changes in my life. They're healthy changes, not self-destructive. I'm here because I want to be here. God has led me here. I'm facing new and as yet unknown developments in my life. But I'm not facing them alone, without God.

My hour is up. I want to do more, but I don't need to. I've heard what I needed to hear right now. My gut tells me so, as does my heart. I got through the first three steps. There are things I'll keep thinking about. For example, I wonder whether I'm also the enemy of God's sheep.

Step Four

Accept the reality of my distorted understanding

A second-grade teacher asked his students to draw a picture of the manger scene where Jesus was born. When they were finished, he hung up the drawings for display. One picture stood out from the rest. It showed a large, roly-poly man sitting next to the baby Jesus and his mother Mary.

The teacher asked the young artist, "Who is that man?"

"Oh," she replied, "That's Round John Virgin!"

We laugh at this obvious misunderstanding of one of our favorite Christmas carols. But we laugh a little nervously. Perhaps we're afraid our own distorted understanding is this visible to everyone around us.

It's one thing to accept our human limitations. It's quite another to accept the reality of our distorted understanding of the Bible. Surely *this* is something we're to transcend. Doesn't coming out of hiding from the Bible mean we're leaving our sin behind? Doesn't friendship with the Bible mean we no longer blame or idolize it, that we've gotten beyond our need to protect it?

Sometimes we take our ability to identify *other* people's distorted understanding as a sign that we no longer hide from the Bible. It's amazingly easy to sit in Bible study and recognize how someone else's understanding of the Bible has been distorted by their hiding. Even though we may not think our own understanding is all that great, we can still point out what's wrong with everyone else's. Sometimes it feels like we're sitting on a high platform, looking down on all the confusion below. Thank God we've been delivered from our blindness and can now see everyone else clearly!

The Bible doesn't invite us to see everyone else. It invites us to see ourselves. But not so we can judge and get rid of our sin. Rather, it invites us to accept our hiding in the same way God accepts it, by looking at ourselves through grace-filled eyes, even as we acknowledge and accept our hiding.

The Bible invites me to accept my hiding. Not to embrace it as a friend, but to accept it as part of the truth about who I am. Like Adam and Eve's, my sin of hiding distorts, twists, and biases my already limited understanding. It affects the way I use my already limited time and resources.

Even after I've clarified what I'm bringing to my friendship with the Bible, and even after I've accepted my limitations as good, my hiding remains. What I discover in the Bible will always reflect not just the goodness of my limitations, but the reality of my need to hide. I will always distort the meaning of the text, sometimes consciously and sometimes unconsciously. My understanding isn't simply limited. Ever since the Fall, it is also distorted. No matter how carefully I read the Bible, I will never sift out the truth as God sees it.

Our prayers for insight sometimes betray our desire to step outside the reality of this fallen world. We ask God to give us undistorted understanding of the Bible. Our prayer is an admission that we have distorted sight right now. But it's also a confession that we haven't accepted that in a fallen world, distorted sight is here to stay. We want God to ignore the Fall, overlook our present sin of hiding, and show us the plain truth. We want God to take us back to a time when human understanding was undistorted by hiding. But according to Genesis and the witness of the entire Bible, that isn't an option in this world.

Sometimes when we pray, we thank God we hold in our hands a book which will give us undistorted sight. But just as the Bible will never give us unlimited understanding, so it will never give us undistorted understanding. The Bible will never give us what the serpent offered Adam and Eve—the ability to see as God sees. In fact, when it's set free to be a witness, the Bible will remind us constantly of the extent of our fallen understanding, even as we search its pages for truth.

The Bible isn't a cure for distorted sight. It's more like a mirror to help us begin recognizing the layers of hiding we've accumulated over the years. Friendship with the Bible can help us discern not just how but *why* we hide. It can encourage us to risk letting go of our hiding places, so our understanding of the Bible and ourselves can change and grow.

It may seem that accepting the reality of our distorted understanding is an admission of failure. No matter how hard we try, we will never understand the Bible. So we may as well give up. No. Distorted understanding isn't the same as total misunderstanding. Even in our most misguided attempts to find meaning in the Bible, there is truth.

Step Four is about learning to recognize our favorite ways of distorting what we read, then going back to see what was correct about even our most obvious misunderstandings. It isn't just about recognizing and letting go of our hiding places. It's also about seeing what was *right* in the way we were looking at the text. If God's truth isn't bound by our understanding, then we should be able to go back, take another look, and discover something true in our interpretations.

This is what it means to see ourselves through grace-filled eyes at the same time that we begin identifying and confessing our patterns of hiding. Each of us has developed favorite ways of avoiding encounter with the Bible. The more sensitive we become to these often unconscious patterns, the more we will recognize the truth that remains even in our misunderstandings of the text.

It may still seem useless to work on these things. If distorted understanding is here to stay, why bother? Perhaps the best way to acknowledge my distorted understanding is to throw my hands up in despair and do nothing at all. Doesn't acceptance mean giving up? Admitting defeat?

Acceptance doesn't mean giving up. In fact, giving up and doing nothing is the *opposite* of acceptance. If I have a chronic illness, accepting that illness means doing whatever is necessary to support my body. Ignoring the illness won't make it go away. Doing nothing is a sure sign I haven't accepted my illness. If I want to be a friend to my body, I will accept and attend to its weaknesses, not just its strengths.

The same is true in Bible study. The most profound sign that I accept the reality of my distorted understanding is regular attention to the way this affects my reading of the Bible. This doesn't mean I give up in despair. It means I take myself seriously, just the way I am.

The exercise that follows will help you attend to your favorite patterns of hiding, so you can discern what is *right* in your understanding of the Bible.

Working it out

1. Consider this hypothetical situation.

It's 11:00 Sunday morning at First Church of Smithville. Sixteen-year-old Mary is sitting with her parents. Mary is frustrated because her parents treat her like an eight-year-old. They just won't let her go, so she can exercise her independence.

She listens as the pastor reads Luke 14:25-35, the sermon text. Verse 26 catches her attention. "If anyone comes to me and does not hate his or her own father and mother, or wife or husband, and children and brothers and sisters, yes, and even his or her own life, that person cannot be my disciple."

2. Now consider the following possibilities. They're ways in which hiding from the Bible might distort Mary's understanding of this passage, given her frustration with her parents.

Mary might *distance* the text. "I'd never say this out loud, but this is one time I'm *glad* I'm not an adult! No way this is about me. I always knew the Bible was out of touch with teenagers. Can you imagine teenagers taking this seriously?"

She might *blame* it because it's difficult to understand. "This teaching is confusing, totally absurd, and immoral! There must be a mistake somewhere. How could Jesus, who commanded us to love each other, tell us to hate one another? This sure isn't what I needed to hear today! Neither did my parents. They already hate my guts. If I were to follow this teaching, they would probably kick me out of the house. I need answers, not more problems!"

She might try to *protect* the Bible by fixing it. "Jesus couldn't possibly mean I'm to hate my parents. He must be overstating it. Exaggerating, so we'll get the *real* point—that we're supposed to put God first in our lives."

Or, Mary might *idolize* the text. "Wow! Maybe this is

the solution I've been looking for! Maybe I need to get really serious about following Jesus and leave home. Maybe it's not so bad that I hate my parents after all!"

3. The point of this exercise isn't to expose and judge your distorted understanding, but to help you see how you can accept it. Go back to Mary's possible responses to Luke 14:26. Can you see how, in spite of hiding from the Bible, she wouldn't be totally wrong about the meaning of the text? Can you identify what might be *right* about her responses? Here are a few suggestions.

—Mary would be right to expect the Bible to say something about parent-child relationships, including her own. Jesus is clearly commenting on them in this passage, though Mary doesn't see this yet.

—This passage *does* give help about how she is to get along with her parents. She's to think of her relationship to them as part of her discipleship with Jesus.

—It's true that Jesus doesn't have her precise situation in mind. It's also true that living as a disciple of Jesus will complicate things with her parents. It will add another person to the relationship. Mary, her mother, her father, and Jesus. If three's a crowd, four could be disaster! If Mary wants to follow Jesus, this text is about her as a disciple of Jesus, not as a disciple of her parents.

—It's true that the word *hate* may not mean here what Mary understands. If hate means she is to throw stones at her parents, ridicule them, despise them, dishonor or kill them, then she's right. The Bible would be wrong. And she would be better off not reading it at all.

4. Now look at the passage *you've* chosen. Be as honest as you can about ways your own hiding from the Bible might distort your understanding of the text. How might your own tendency to blame, distance, protect, or idolize the Bible be visible in the way you understand the text? Write it down! (If you need further examples, review chapter two.)

5. Look once more at your first responses to the text. Can you see what's right about them? Write it down! Compare your understanding of the text now with your initial understanding of it. Have you made any progress?

What this looks like

(Psalm 23, continued from previous chapters)

I had earlier spent time on this psalm. But it wouldn't leave me alone. I decided to see what Step Four might look like. How might I be hiding from this psalm? This time I was more flexible about how long I spent, though I kept it under an hour each of the two days I worked on it. I checked in with myself each day, keeping track of what was happening in my life and how I was feeling. Then I reviewed my earlier notes on this passage before beginning the exercise. Here's a summary of what was going on each day.

On the first day I was feeling pretty calm and was looking forward to a family dinner at one of our favorite restaurants. My son was bringing a friend who was staying with us for a few nights. I was still fearful about changes coming in my life, but I knew what I needed to do next and had spent time working on some of my personal issues.

On the second day I had just gone through a difficult family conversation that arose during our dinner at the restaurant. During the discussion I felt confused and out of touch with some of my family. I didn't feel what they were feeling. I kept thinking of Psalm 23 during our sometimes intense conversation. I knew God had prepared this table for me, though I wasn't sure who the enemy was. I felt as though we were all the enemy in ways we only partially understood.

I was sad and disappointed that the dinner wasn't more pleasant, but I was also calm. It was difficult to describe how I was feeling, partly because I was confused, but partly because I feel more comfortable talking about ideas than about myself. The discussion ended on a tentatively positive note and we agreed to talk later this week. I was anxious about the coming conversation.

1. As I pondered the example about Mary in church with her parents, I couldn't help thinking how difficult family matters are, and how equally difficult many Bible passages about family matters seem to be. When I first looked at Psalm 23 this week, I did it out of personal distress. But now I felt calm about my personal situation, and some family matters were coming up. Psalm 23 suddenly looked like a text about family matters. I haven't usually thought of it this way.

2. and 3. I had no notes on these steps in the exercise.

4. and 5. How might I be hiding from Psalm 23? And what was right about my initial interpretation of it? Here are my notes, written on two successive days, (a) before and (b) after our family discussion in the restaurant.

a. My first thought is that in the past I've idealized this psalm. I've made it into a picturesque pastoral scene with little connection to the real world. I don't think I did that when I worked on it a few days ago. But my earliest associations with this psalm encouraged a romantic mind-set in which I was always the beloved sheep. I think I've distanced this psalm not just from real life, but from the truth about me. In seeing myself as the perpetual sheep (which, in one sense, I am), I've tended to see whoever I thought was opposing me on any given day as the enemy of verse 4.

I now know that sometimes I am my worst enemy. Also, people who seem to be my enemies may, in fact, become friends. Not so much because of changes in them, as because of changes in me. I've also pictured this table sitting in full view of my enemies. They were sitting around the edges, looking on while God treated me as though I were a favorite child. But the table is in the presence of my enemies. The text seems to leave open the possibility that I am seated with my enemies. Indeed, I may not even be aware they are my enemies.

More difficult is the realization that my so-called enemies may be quoting this psalm just as I do. And they may consider me to be their enemy. The psalm doesn't say they are God's enemies! If I obstruct their need to follow God, instead of following me, for example, I am at least enemy-like. The point I'm getting at is that each of us has God as our shepherd, and God will be the best shepherd possible for each of us. This psalm is a personal confession. But if I make it simply my personal confession, I miss part of the meaning. It can also be, for example, my daughter's personal confession. God is her best shepherd, too.

What's right about my initial interpretation of the psalm? Even though the psalm isn't my personal possession and I'm not always a grateful sheep, it's good to hear it as the story of my life. Only because I've experienced it as the story of my life do I have confidence that it is also the story of my daughter's life. And my son's, his friend's, and my husband's life.

A second thing comes to mind that might involve hiding from this text. I've used this psalm as a kind of magic wand in the past, especially when I was a young child, but also as an adult. I've quoted the opening line when I've been in fearful situations. Like having to go into dark rooms in our house to get something for my parents. Or getting up at night and seeing my reflection in the mirror, without any lights on in the room. Or worse. When the fear and adrenalin got going I found that silently repeating the opening line of Psalm 23 calmed me down and gave me courage. It didn't take away my fear forever. It just got me through the hard spots in life.

I know that in those moments I gave the first verse of this psalm magical, godlike power. Not just to calm me down, but also to protect me like an invisible shield. But I was hurt anyway, sometimes in the very situations in which I quoted the verse over and over to myself. Psalm 23:1 wasn't a genie inside a bottle, available to make everything turn out right.

Nonetheless, I'm not willing to say my childhood use of this psalm was a form of hiding. It was a survival skill that served me well. Today my understanding of life and of the Bible have changed. I know that quotes from the Bible aren't magic wands that will change reality. Life is hard and it isn't always fair. But I still quote the opening lines of Psalm 23 when I'm in stressful situations. The Lord is my shepherd, and I am God's sheep. I won't make it alone, without God in my life. My childhood intuition about this psalm was right.

b. I've distanced this psalm by not identifying myself with the enemy, and by assuming the enemy was always sinister and evil, lurking on the outside, watching for a chance to grab a sheep. The last twenty-four hours were incredibly difficult, but I see something else I hadn't seen before. We were sitting around a table at the restaurant, and I wasn't sure who the enemy was. None of us wanted to be the enemy. We wanted to have fun together. I know from our discussion that each of us has painful family issues to face, and that we're not all in the same place. But God is the shepherd for each of us.

What I now see is that I'm not the enemy, as long as I'm allowing God to be their shepherd and mine. Maybe the enemies of verse 4 are false shepherds, not wolves or other sinister animals. Maybe they're people just like I am whenever I try to take over the role of God as Shepherd, instead of letting God do what only God does best. I can't solve my family members' personal issues. I'm not their shepherd. To attempt to figure out what's best for them right now is to make myself into an enemy, a false shepherd.

I'm reminded of sermons about how dumb sheep are. Psalm 23 isn't about dumb sheep. But it *is* pretty ludicrous to imagine that sheep could lead other sheep beside still waters, or into right paths. What's right about those sermons is that sheep do well when they remember they're sheep, not the shepherd.

Step Five

Accept that the Bible won't always seem to be my friend

The world of spies and counterspies is intriguing because you're never sure which people are friends and which are enemies. In James Bond movies the hero always hides out as a friend of the enemy for so long and so well, that the spy begins to accept this pretend world as real. Then there's the shock of going home and discovering that old friends and true patriots appear enemy-like and threatening.

The Bible is an old friend. Sometimes it looks like an enemy because I've been hiding from it for so long that I've forgotten what this old friend looks like. When I finally allow it to do its work as a witness, it often sounds and feels more like an enemy than a friend. Instead of encountering it as a means of grace, I may experience it as an unwelcome intrusion into my life, a source of embarrassment, or a means of harsh judgment.

A friend once reported to me that one of my enemies said I was difficult to confront. I didn't like this. I didn't like hearing what this other person had said behind my back. I didn't like my friend repeating it to me. But most of all I didn't like it when I asked if she agreed, then watched her search for subtle, "friendly" ways of saying that yes, she did agree. In moments like this our friends seem to have joined forces with the enemy.

Sometimes the Bible appears to belong to the camp of the enemy. It seems to have joined forces with people who think they understand me and know what I need. But the Bible isn't all those people. And it isn't a weapon. It doesn't belong to other people any more than it belongs to me.

The Bible is a witness to the truth about God and God's world. If it were my enemy it would treat me the way I often treat it. It would hide the truth from me instead of revealing it. It would seek to mislead or deceive me. It would distance itself from me, protect me from the truth about myself, pretend I am more than human, and agree with my harsh judgment of myself and other people. But the Bible doesn't hide from me, even though I sometimes wish it would.

Like a broken record, the Bible reminds me on every page of the goodness of my limited understanding, and of the extent to which my sin has distorted that understanding. It does this by telling story after story about people who seem to live in a different world than I do. It presents me with hard sayings and difficult passages one after the other. And it never even offers to answer all of my questions. The Bible spreads before me its complexity, including all the things I don't like about it. It makes itself vulnerable to being misunderstood because of its limitations. It doesn't *distance* me; it waits for me to draw near. It waits for me to ask how this book is the story of my life.

The Bible doesn't transport me to some other world in which human beings don't have to risk being seen just as they are. Nor does it offer false comfort by pretending everything will be all right if I just step out of hiding. It doesn't tell me of people who worked out their salvation without fear and trembling. And it isn't about people living happily ever after. It reminds me on every page that life is hard, and that we humans make it even harder when we try to escape our limitations or deny our sin. The Bible doesn't *protect* me from the truth about life. Sometimes I wish it would.

The Bible refuses to go along with my desire to play God. I keep trying to position myself on the outside of the human race, looking down on all those sinners and misguided people who don't do things according to *my* will. But the Bible keeps reminding me that I'm not on the outside. I'm on the inside. I belong to the human race. I don't belong on the outside, fighting and plotting against all God's enemies. The Bible reminds me on every page that *God* is in control and that God often works through people I would rather fight or ignore. The Bible never lets me forget that I do not know the mind or the ways of God in this fallen world. In all its stories it offers me only one role—being human. The Bible doesn't *idolize* me. Sometimes this sounds like bad news. I like to pretend I'm God.

Finally, no matter how far I fall, the Bible never gives me the satisfaction of agreeing with my harsh, relentless judgment of myself or of others. This doesn't mean the Bible overlooks sin. In fact, it holds up a mirror and asks me to see myself in every human being who appears on its pages, including Jesus Christ. It knows me better than I know myself. The Bible also invites me to look at myself and others in the way that God looks at me. I may judge myself and others to be insignificant, worthless, and beyond hope of salvation.

But according to the Bible, God has another opinion. From beginning to end, the Bible is the story of God disagreeing with me, not the story of God accusing me. God doesn't say it's all my fault; neither does the Bible. The Bible doesn't *blame* me. Even this can sound like bad news. I may be miserable and I may make life miserable for people around me, but sometimes I would rather punish myself and others, than change.

Perhaps you've followed this process faithfully, but right now you like the Bible or some parts of it even less than before you started. This isn't a sign the process has broken down. In fact, this may be precisely what needed to happen. It may be a sign that you need to examine the text more carefully, keeping an open mind.

The Bible is a means of grace. It conveys life, not death. If I believe the Bible is my friend, perhaps it feels like an enemy right now because of something in *me*. Until I hear the passage I'm studying as *good* news, I haven't yet connected fully with the witness of the Bible. The exercise that follows suggests a few ways to take another look at the Bible and the way you're hearing it right now.

Working it out

1. Using the passage you've chosen for these exercises, make a list of things you don't like about the text. List things you find boring, trivial, needlessly repetitive, disturbing, threatening, frightening, infuriating, or just plain wrong.

2. State as clearly as you can *why* these things affect you in this way on this particular day, or at this particular time of your life.

> —Perhaps things you don't like about this text reflect things you don't like in yourself or in your history. If so, what are they? Write them down.
> —Perhaps the text doesn't seem to agree with your present view of what's going on in your

life. What *is* the difference between your point of view and what you understand as the text's point of view? Write it down.

—Perhaps there's some other reason. What is it?

3. Assuming the text is *not* your enemy, what might it be inviting you to do?

—Accept something about yourself or your history as part of who you are?

—Change your present view of what's really going on in your life, or in the world?

—Keep an open mind, until you understand the text better?

—Move into unknown territory?

—Change how you relate to yourself or others?

4. If the Bible still seems more enemy than friend, put your notes away for now. But before you do, write down a time when you'll work on this passage again. Take as long as you need, but promise yourself you'll work on it again. The reason it seems an enemy may have to do with you, not with the Bible.

What this looks like

(Psalm 23 continued from previous chapters)

When I decided to try Step Five, I was pretty sure I wouldn't find anything I didn't like in Psalm 23. But after checking in with myself and reviewing my notes, I recognized something that troubled me. First, here's a summary of what was happening the day I worked on this step.

I felt sad and subdued after a long talk with one of my children. I listened to what it felt like growing up, and could hear in my child's story many themes that run through my own story. I felt some despair about the past; I wondered whether all I could now count on was the present. I wanted to take away the pain my child suffered growing up. I was sad because I hadn't recognized the depth of this pain when things were tough back then. I was also grateful I've changed since then, so that I now hear more clearly. Now here are some of my notes.

1. I'm disturbed by the shepherd imagery in this psalm.

2. I find shepherd imagery disturbing and even threatening. Even though this psalm is about God who is my shepherd, I am reminded as I read it now of human beings who have tried to be my shepherd. I know the Bible sometimes speaks of leaders as shepherds. Some humans have tried to be God to me, under the cover of thinking themselves shepherds. Sometimes I wish this image weren't even in the Bible, even though it brings me comfort and encourages me to keep putting one foot in front of the other.

On this particular day I'm aware of a family tradition that says parents know best. When my children were growing up, I sometimes thought I knew best what they needed, what they should feel or think, what they should do next. I haven't always been a human shepherd to my children. I've sometimes tried to take on a superhuman, godlike role in their upbringing. Something in me wants to blame the Bible for even leaving the door open to this interpretation of what it means to be a shepherd.

3. I think this psalm is inviting me to accept my past. It does this by telling me God follows behind me with goodness and mercy. Even though I can't change the past, God still inhabits my past and my children's past. I don't have to keep going back and wishing it weren't so, pretending it was better than it was, or trying to identify and destroy my enemies.

Psalm 23 invites me to accept God's goodness and mercy in the working out of my past. I don't need to fear the evil of the past. I can look it straight in the eyes and accept it as part of who I am today. Sometimes I feel the urge to take over God's job, just like some of the adults in my life tried to take over God's job in relation to me. Insofar as they were false shepherds, they remind me of myself. This, too, is part of my identity.

Step Six

Include others in the process

Last week I got into a heated discussion with a woman in my Bible study. We didn't agree at all about the meaning of the text we were working on. The discussion was intense; I knew there was no easy way to end the exchange.

So I said rather feebly, "Oh well. At least we had a chance to get to know each other better."

She replied immediately and with great vigor, "We certainly did! In fact, that's the *only* reason I came to Bible study tonight. I wanted to check you out!"

This may be our greatest fear about coming to Bible study. Other people are there just to check us out. Unfortunately, some of them probably are.

This step invites you to include others in the process of making friends with the Bible. Although Bible study isn't the only way to do this, we urge you to give it a try. There are other settings in which people talk about what the Bible means. This happens frequently on youth outings, mission trips, and in church or seminary groups that gather informally. It isn't necessary to have the actual text in our hands every time we discuss it.

But it *is* important to have the actual text in our hands or immediately available some of the time. Otherwise we're just studying our memories of the Bible. If we're going to make friends with the Bible, we need to become acquainted with the text itself. Human friendships don't flourish on nothing but memories and hearsay. Neither does friendship with the Bible. That's why we urge you to think of Bible study groups as the setting in which you'll work on this part of the process.

Steps One through Five were about things you could do in your personal study and reflection on the Bible. This is crucial, since most of us depend on other peoples' thoughts and feelings about what's going on in the Bible. We don't take time or think it's legitimate to make up our own minds about what the Bible may mean. But the Bible is given to everyone, not just experts. Each of us must take seriously our personal work with the Bible.

At the same time, this personal work is just part of the process. I must find my own voice and risk deciding what I think and feel about the Bible. But I must also allow the Bible to have its own voice in the process. I must let it speak for itself. Otherwise I may simply hear my own voice in the text, as though I were talking to myself. I may miss what the Bible wants me to hear today.

We believe the Bible has a voice of its own. It doesn't need us to defend or speak for it. It can hold up its end of the conversation. But the Bible is a written text, not a living person. One way to allow the written text to speak for itself is to allow other people to speak for themselves about what *they* hear in the Bible.

In human relationships we depend on full, open discussion to clarify issues. We don't assume that any one person is capable of seeing every side of an issue. By listening to a variety of voices and contributing our part to the discussion, we gain perspectives none of us had in the beginning.

Similarly, if we want to broaden our understanding of the Bible, we must listen to other perspectives and be willing to share our own. Only in this way do we free the Bible to speak for itself. When we listen to others and share our own thoughts and feelings, we relinquish our need to control what the Bible says as well as how and to whom it speaks. We allow the Bible its own voice.

We can't understand the Bible in isolation from other people. Some of us wish we could. We hate asking for help. We feel awkward admitting there are things we don't understand, especially when everyone else seems to get the point and wants to move on to something else. We tell ourselves it would be better to stay at home and work on this by ourselves. Then we wouldn't be so much trouble to the group.

But this won't work. The nature of the Bible itself requires that we listen to each other to understand Scripture. The Bible wasn't given to isolated individuals or to small groups of experts. It was given to all of us together.

Sometimes we think that if we find just the right Bible teacher or Bible study leader, everything will be clear. We pin all our hopes on the leader of the group. Then we're disappointed when he or she doesn't meet our expectations. But we don't need just the right teacher or leader. We need each other; we need each person God brings into our group.

The way we were created confirms this. Just as Adam and Eve needed each other from the beginning, so we need each other in the process of making friends with the Bible. Adam and Eve's need for each other was good. Our need for each other as we befriend the Bible is *good*. It isn't shameful or a sign that our understanding is inferior. This is the way God made us, and it is good.

Further, just as God brought Adam the very person he needed, so God brings to us just the people who will deepen our friendship with the Bible. We don't need to go on big searches for them. They're already present, just waiting for us to discover them. We need them and they need us, just as Adam and Eve equally needed each other. We need each other, with all our insights and confusion, to broaden our understanding of the Bible.

We need each other—but we avoid this step at all costs. It raises our urge to hide not just from the Bible but from each other. We're afraid to let people know what we're thinking and feeling about the Bible. They may not like what they hear. Worse, they may decide they don't like *us*.

For many of us Step Six may be the most difficult. Attending Bible study regularly is a start. But just going to Bible study won't guarantee we're involving others in this process. This step isn't about going to Bible study. It's about what *happens* during Bible study.

Small group Bible study can be fearsome. No matter how well I've prepared myself to lead the group, I'm never quite ready for the anxiety that rises in me just before we begin. I'm tempted to take firm control and in dictator-like fashion fill the time with information about the text. Then no one, including me, would have to talk out loud about what the text might mean. In a moment of honesty and desperation, one church member who refuses to attend Bible study summed it all up: "There's absolutely nothing I want to do less in my life than sit around with a group of people and discuss what I think the Bible says!"

Bible study is an intense experience because it demands that at least some of us expose to the rest of the group our thoughts and feelings about what we see in the text. When we gather for Bible study we must interpret the text. It isn't enough to be able to repeat the content of the

Bible, or turn to familiar passages. Since the Bible can be interpreted in many ways, it's essential that we risk letting each other hear and consider our different interpretations and why we believe they are important. Sometimes this will feel wrong, or even disrespectful. It may create tension. But if we're going to understand better what's going on in the Bible, we must risk exposing what we *think* might be going on.

This isn't easy, so we've developed some avoidance techniques just for Bible study. They help us hide not just from the Bible but from involvement with each other. For example, we may read the Bible selectively, talking only about what we think we already understand and agree on. We may avoid difficult sayings, since talking about them might make us look like beginners. On the other hand, we may love these difficult passages. Since everyone knows no one understands them, it's relatively safe to say what we think they mean.

Some of us prefer silence. We're more than willing to let others risk making their observations while we retreat into the safety of silence. We may refuse to enter into the discussion, protesting that we learn more by listening than by speaking. Or we may work up enough courage to break our silence, but only after we've prepared carefully packaged remarks that shift attention away from us. We already know we'll become visible in our comments or questions, so we try to say just enough to insure we'll be seen as we want to be seen.

Many of us would rather do anything than risk ridicule or rejection. So we sometimes hide behind the Bible itself. We resort to phrases like, "This is what the Bible says" to avoid saying, "This is what I *think* the Bible means, and here's why."

We substitute the words of the Bible for our own words, as though the Bible's words were self-explanatory.

We quote comforting and familiar verses, instead of exposing our own disturbing, unfamiliar thoughts and feelings about what we hear in the Bible. We're not ready to let other people see what we're really thinking and feeling about the Bible, much less what we think and feel about what's going on in the group.

You may choose to stop here. If so, we invite you to read on and consider the possibility of continuing the process later. This step is crucial since the Bible doesn't invite us simply to get to know its pages better. It also invites us, in the very process of knowing the Bible better, to know each other better. To omit this step is to cheat ourselves of a gift the Bible offers us.

We don't have an exercise (or an example) for this step since it can't be approached in a step-by-step fashion. Instead, we have a checklist. The checklist assumes you're attending a Bible study. It will help you know when you're avoiding involvement with people in your Bible study. It will also help you stay on track and recognize your progress. The checklist focuses on what's happening with *you* during Bible study, not on what's happening with others in the group. This is because getting together to study the Bible isn't an opportunity to become judgmental. It's an opportunity to listen and share, so that everyone hears the Bible more clearly.

Working it out

Here are questions to ask yourself from time to time.

1. When I come to Bible study, am I prepared? Have I worked on the first part of this process (Steps One through Five)?

2. Am I open about my own understanding of the text, and my own response to it?

3. Do I give others time to explain what they think the

text means, and to express their own feelings about the text? Do I do this willingly, even when I don't agree with them, or think they're confused or unclear?

4. How do I respond when I hear other people hiding from the Bible by blaming, distancing, idolizing, or protecting it? Do I feel the need to correct them? If so, why? What am I trying to avoid?

5. What am I learning about my own favorite ways of hiding from the Bible? What are they? What am I trying to avoid when I hide in these ways?

6. Which members of the group seem to be my enemies right now? What don't I like about them? What does my response to them show me about *myself* right now?

7. What new insights have I had into the text since I've been including others in the process?

8. Have I been tempted to stop working on this step? If so, why? What does this tell me about *myself*?

9. How willing am I to continue working on this step—even though it means taking risks and living with some uncertainty about how my understanding of the Bible and how my relationships to the people in my group might change? If I'm hesitant, what am I afraid might happen (be specific)?

Step Seven

Count on God's presence in this process

For several years I regularly attended a church Bible study. Then I moved away, returning to visit two or three times a year. It was always wonderful to see my old friends and to find that new members were still joining.

But after a few visits I began to notice a pattern. No matter which passage in the Bible was being studied, the same old battle lines were being drawn. On the surface people seemed to be debating the meaning of the text. Yet I knew many of them personally and could tell they were actually fighting about long-standing differences among themselves. Sometimes a newcomer would ask a question or try to make a comment. But the discussion quickly returned to the safe old standoffs.

I recognized myself in my friends. I used to think Bible study was about someone winning. Winning meant expressing vigorously and arguing persuasively for the viewpoint that seemed most acceptable to the church, or to certain members of the group. I was a good fighter. It was important to score points and to sound sure of myself. I knew I had a lot to lose if my interpretations were rejected. This wasn't just about the Bible. It was about how I lived my life.

Even the most well-intentioned Bible study sometimes becomes an arena of struggle. Instead of working together to discover meaning in the text, group members wrestle with each other for *control* of meaning in the text. We think that if we control the meaning of a text, we can influence or even control other people. The Bible becomes a tool or weapon to change other people's thoughts, feelings, or actions.

Sadly, the best fighters among us know too well the damaging consequences of these tactics. Other people have misused the Bible on us, trying to control what we were allowed to think, feel, and do. Some of us are still fighting back.

No wonder we hesitate to include others in the process of befriending the Bible. Left to ourselves, we would devour one another. Bible study isn't necessarily a place of refuge.

From the beginning the Bible speaks to our fear of including others in the process. It lets us know there's more going on in Bible study than meets the eye. The first chapters of the Bible aren't just the story of Adam and Eve. They are the story of Adam and Eve and *God*. God is the third party in their relationship, just as God is the third party in *every* human relationship.

And as Adam and Eve weren't left to their own devices in the Garden, so we aren't left to our own devices when we meet for Bible study. Their story invites us to think of Bible study as a place where God is acknowledged openly as the third party in every encounter.

The Bible confirms what we already know from experience. We know it isn't enough to count simply on ourselves or on the human beings God brings into our lives. We need each other. But we also need God. The Bible is the history of God with us.

We need God's presence in a special way when we risk letting other people know what we're thinking and feeling about the Bible or what we think it means for us. For some, the risk will come in *not* spending so much time letting people know everything there is to know about our thoughts, feelings, and ideas. In either case we won't become truly involved with other people in the group unless we count on God's presence. God is as present as the person sitting next to us.

Step Seven is the other side of Step Six. It's also the other side of Steps One through Five. I would never get to the point of including others in my study of the Bible if God were not with me from the beginning. Step Seven doesn't introduce God into this process. It just acknowledges what is already true about *all* life. It invites me to act on this truth intentionally whenever I gather with others for Bible study.

If I'm going to count on God's presence, it's important to know what God's presence *doesn't* mean. This isn't easy, since we like to think of God as our problem solver. Perhaps this step will also invite you to reconsider your understanding of God.

God's presence in Bible study doesn't mean—
>   —the end of conflict, or of power struggles within the group;
>   —the end of confusion or ambiguity about what the text means, or about what's going on in the group;
>   —we won't be dismayed by our human limitations;
>   —our understanding of the Bible will no longer be distorted;
>   —we'll never be disappointed about our Bible study, or that it will always be a smashing success;

—no one will ever feel hurt, misunderstood, or ignored.

To sum it up, counting on God's presence doesn't mean our problems with the text or with each other will magically disappear. In fact, it may sometimes seem the opposite has happened. It may feel as though we've just opened Pandora's box.

It may seem God's presence isn't worth very much. But consider the following ways we've experienced God's presence with us in Bible study.

Counting on God's presence means knowing God is with us not just while we're together but before and after we meet. This is true even if we change Bible studies, decide not to attend for a while, or drop out. God's work in us doesn't begin or end when Bible study begins and ends.

Counting on God's presence means knowing God is for everyone in the group. God doesn't take my side against you, or your side against me. I can't claim to have God on *my* side, as though God were a weapon of warfare, or as though Bible study were about winners and losers. God isn't the possession of any one person or group of people.

It means *God* is in charge of what happens next. Whether we take the risk of opening our mouths or of keeping them closed, we don't control the outcome. God does.

It means God doesn't judge us harshly if we choose not to share our thoughts and feelings about the Bible. Nor does God keep a record of how often we monopolize the discussion. God knows it's difficult to include others in this process.

It means God alone has the big picture of what's going on in our group and of what's best for each of us. God alone knows who needs to be here today and which messages you and I, singly and together, need to hear from this text.

It means God can defend God's good name. We don't need to protect God from misunderstanding.

In sum, counting on God's presence means I'm free to focus on myself and listen for things *I* need to hear not just as an individual but as a group member. I don't need to act as God's representative or decide which other person in the group might fill this role. Nor am I responsible for the success of the Bible study. I am responsible only for my personal contribution and full participation as a member of the group. I can relax and enjoy the process even though I may sometimes find it painful.

It's impossible to leave God outside the door when we meet for Bible study. But it *is* possible to omit this final step. Knowing God is present isn't the same as counting on God's presence. If we don't count on God's presence, certain consequences will follow.

First, Step Six as we've described it will be impossible to carry out. We may make it through Steps One through Five, and we may learn a lot about ourselves and the Bible in the process. But Step Six is different. It is a fearful thing to fall into the hands of living people!

Second, we will be spectators in the group rather than participants. We'll be present in the room, but we won't be connected personally to the life-changing energy of God. God will still be with us, and our presence will be important. But we'll be on the outside, looking in. Sometimes we won't understand what all the excitement is about.

Finally, we may learn a lot about the Bible and about other people in the group, but we won't learn to trust the Bible and other members of the group as friends. We won't be willing to risk letting them challenge and invite us to change our thoughts and feelings not just toward them and the Bible but toward God as well. And we won't experience the joy of having someone gratefully acknowledge that we contributed to their change and growth.

As with Step Six, we don't have an exercise to work through in a step-by-step fashion. That's because God's presence with us isn't something we control. We can, however, signal our willingness to count on God in this process. We can take concrete steps to demonstrate our belief that God is indeed present and in control of the outcome of our Bible study. The following checklist will help assess your progress in consciously including God in the process of making friends with the Bible.

Working it out

Here are some questions to ask yourself from time to time.

1. Am I making progress on Steps One through Five? Am I consciously counting on God's presence throughout this entire process, even though I may not be aware of God's presence?

2. Am I making progress on Step Six? Am I learning to include others in the process? The extent of my willingness to include others in the process is directly related to my willingness to count on God in the entire process.

3. Do I sometimes pretend I'm God? Am I learning to let go of my need to be in control of the group, or of what members of the group think and feel about the Bible?

—Do I feel a need to be right?

—Do I feel a need to defend the Bible, or to correct what I find to be unacceptable interpretations or feelings?

—Do I feel a need to defend God from misunderstanding?

—Do I think I understand others better than they understand themselves?

—Do I think I know what's best for the group? Or who really should have been here today?

—Where might I consider making some changes?

How much change feels comfortable to me right now? What might I do differently next time?

4. Do I sometimes pretend someone else in the group is God? Do I give others in the group power to decide or limit what I ought to hear in the Bible or how I should feel about it?

—Do I find myself quickly accepting what others say about the text, without considering what *I* think and feel about it?

—Do I keep quiet most of the time, going along with what others say?

—Do I have inner conversations with other members of the group, instead of public conversations? If so, why? Is it because I believe they know the Bible better than I? Maybe it's because I'm afraid to hear my own voice. Or because I feel ashamed of how little I seem to know.

—Do I leave Bible study wishing I had spoken up instead of being so quiet? Am I resentful because others in the group seem to dominate the conversation? What seems to keep me from speaking?

—Do I ever risk speaking first, or contributing to what seems a private discussion between two or three other group members? If not, why not?

—Where might it be time to make some changes? How much change feels comfortable to me right now? What might I do differently next time?

Postscript to Part II

Here's a brief overview of the process we've been describing. You may find it useful after you've become familiar with each exercise. We've included it to give you a sense for the entire process and to show there's nothing mysterious about these exercises. They're made up of simple, everyday questions. At the same time, there aren't just two or three questions. There are many, arranged in a particular order.

Step One: Getting in touch with myself
—What's happening?
—What will I read?
—How have I heard it interpreted?
—What stands out?
—How does this connect with what's happening?
—What are my fears?

Step Two: Accepting my limitations
—How much time do I have?
—What don't I understand?

—What resources do I have?
—Which resources might I actually use?
—How much time have I spent?

Step Three: Accepting the Bible just as it is
—What will I work on first, *without* outside resources?
—What do I understand better?
—What do I still want to work on?
—How do my outside resources help?
—What would I say differently?
—What is and isn't the text about?
—How does this connect with what's happening?

Step Four: Thinking about hiding
—How have I hidden from this text?
—What was right about my early understanding?
—How has my understanding changed?

Step Five: Taking another look
—What don't I like?
—Why don't I like it, given my present situation?
—What might the text be asking of me?
—Does it still sound like an enemy?
—If so, when will I work on it again?

Step Six: Including others
—What am I learning in Bible study about myself?
—How has my understanding of the text changed?
—What might happen if I continue coming to Bible study?

Step Seven: Counting on God's presence
—How have I counted on God's presence in this process?
—How might I count on God even more?
—What changes am I willing to make?

PART III:
Examples from our Journals

Introduction

Whenever I read students' seminary papers my favorite question is, "What does this *look* like?" This part of the book is our way of showing you several more times what making friends with the Bible looks like. We'll be using familiar passages from different parts of the Bible. We invite you to take out your Bibles and follow along as we work through the first five steps.

We haven't included reports of our work with Steps Six and Seven, mainly because we had no ongoing group Bible study that was working on the texts we chose for this book.

Each of us has led and participated in Bible studies while writing this book. Sometimes we've led in the spirit of the checklists that follow Steps Six and Seven, inviting participants to attend to the concerns covered in them. We've also used the questions to check our own attitudes and behaviors. We invite you to make the checklists a regular part of your personal preparation for group Bible study, even though your group may not use them.

The following three examples are taken almost directly from our journals, with explanations along the way as needed. We've included a substantial amount of personal material to illustrate how we make connections between our lives and the text. We've also omitted some details to honor privacy.

Luke 2:1-20

(from Elouise's journal)

Step One: Getting in touch with myself

My feelings were mixed the day I began this exercise. On the one hand, I was excited, eagerly anticipating working through this process. I was grateful because my efforts to take better care of my body were paying off. I was also grateful for a conversation I had with my daughter the night before, which left me more confident about her move to another city.

On the other hand, I was fighting the familiar feeling that I am somehow responsible for my children's choices, especially when other people report them to me. Someone had done this the day before, and though I didn't want to, I had begun to feel responsible for something one of my children had chosen not to do.

I was also sad and filled with regret because I had forgotten to call my son on his birthday the day before. I knew I was feeling over-responsible for this family matter, and I resented the way mothers are expected to take initiative for things like this.

I chose to work on Luke 2:1-20. I usually hear this passage read or recited at Christmas. People assume it's about the awesomeness of Jesus' birth, the miracle of Christmas. I've heard sermons on how we must make room in our hearts, homes, and lives for Jesus. The innkeeper has been a well-known character, especially in children's Christmas plays. I've also been invited in sermons to be one of the shepherds, witnessing to all I've seen and heard. Every year I see this text interpreted on Christmas cards and in nativity scenes. It seems to be a text with meaning for Christmas, not so much for the rest of the year. The angels are very visible and almost taken for granted. Of course they were there!

Here's what jumped off the page when I read it through the first time.

—The description of Mary, "to whom he was engaged and who was expecting a child" (v. 5).

—The shepherds are named over and over, directly and indirectly (vv. 8-20).

—The shepherds were living in the fields, not in homes (similar to Jesus; v. 8).

—The shepherds were terrified (v. 9).

—Mary treasured all these words and pondered them in her heart (v. 19).

My first attempt to make connections between what I saw in this text and what was going on in my life produced a huge load of guilt and harsh judgment of myself. The connection seemed to be the celebration of birthdays, even though none of the items I had listed were directly connected to that theme. My son's birthday was the day before. He was out of town. I had forgotten to call. The text seemed to be reminding me that celebrating birthdays is important, and that I had let the moment pass unacknowledged by a phone call. I wished I could order up an angel choir for my son.

I decided to take a break for lunch and come back later. The connection I had made didn't feel comfortable. It didn't seem connected to what had stood out in the text the first time I read it. In addition, no matter how I approached it, the text still seemed too familiar, too "Christmasy."

In the evening I tried again. I focused on my list of things that had jumped out at me. This time the connection was crystal clear. I connected with Mary as a mother. Mary didn't seem to be getting a very smooth start at the business of mothering. But she knew how to listen, how to treasure what was told her about her son.

In some ways, 2:19 seemed the most human verse in the whole account. Maybe Mary had to mother Jesus before she felt ready. She is presented as a very human figure in this story. Young, vulnerable to public misunderstanding and ridicule, not giving birth in the best of circumstances. I felt my humanity as a mother very keenly the day I began working on this passage.

My worst fears about this text were the same I have with any familiar text. I was afraid I wouldn't discover anything new or fresh. I was afraid it would remain a relatively harmless and sentimental Christmas text, despite the connections I had just identified.

Step Two: Accepting my limitations
I decided to work about an hour a day on this text. I planned at first to be done in a few days, but ended up spending four days on the text, spread over a period of eight days. As I went along, I found myself spending an hour to an hour and a half on the text each of the four days.

Here are things I didn't understand in the story.

—What historical, political, and cultural data would help me better understand Joseph and Mary's situation? What does "registration" mean (The King

James Version says "taxed")? Who are the officials named (Emperor Augustus and Quirinius the governor of Syria); why does Luke include their names in this account?

—I'd like to know more about shepherds. What were they like? How did they live? Why did the angel and the heavenly host come to *them*?

—2:10 speaks of good news for all people, while 2:14 speaks of "peace among those whom he favors." Does this mean all people will be granted peace, or just "those whom he favors"? What does "favors" mean in this setting?

—Why does 2:19 begin with "but"? Why doesn't it just say "and" Mary treasured all these words? Why is Mary's response named separately from that of all the others who heard the shepherds?

I decided to use *The International Standard Bible Encyclopedia* (*ISBE*) as my resource for this text and any others I might work on as examples for this book. I didn't want to spend a lot of time checking outside resources, since this would defeat a major purpose of this book. I wanted a resource that would give relatively up-to-date insight into historical and cultural background without going into great detail about the meaning of texts.

Step Three: Accepting the Bible just as it is

I returned to the text after not looking at it for a day. Before beginning Step Three, I took about ten minutes to write down what was going on in my life, and how I was feeling that day. I also reflected briefly on my connection to the text.

I had spent the day before in the midst of mother work. I helped my daughter get ready to move, did what I could to be supportive, and spent more time than usual just listening and talking. I found myself ready for her to be on her way because I could hear *she* was ready.

This wasn't the only change in my normal routine. I had also made three trips to the repair shop before my car was properly repaired. It felt like a bizarre day. I spent time on the car that I didn't think I had, and I ended up spending more money than I thought I had. Late in the afternoon I discovered an error in the checkbook, an error in my favor. I was relieved, grateful, and annoyed all at the same time. For weeks I had been increasingly anxious about how we would manage to help two children with their school finances. I still didn't have all the answers, but I began to trust things would work out.

I also talked with a friend I hadn't seen for several weeks. She helped me see the good that had been happening all month right in the middle of what had often felt discouraging. Some of the most difficult times for me as a mother could be seen as signs of growth, not failure. They were signs that I was relating to my family in healthy ways. It felt difficult because we were all changing, trying out new behaviors with each other.

Talking to my friend was like having an angel appear to point out the miracle that was happening in my family relationships. I was feeling strongly connected to Luke 2. This text was about a mother in a real family. A mother who also needed special messengers to point out the miracle happening in *her* family, right in the midst of difficult, uncomfortable, and unexpected circumstances.

When I started working on Step Three I didn't pay attention to the instructions, which asked me not to consult any outside resources yet. Instead, I began working right away in my Bible encyclopedia, reading the entries on Augustus and on Quirinius. I didn't take many notes, but found myself getting bogged down anyway. My initial connection with the text didn't seem to be going anywhere, even though I was finding some helpful insights.

Among other things, I learned that Augustus, the first Roman emperor, was a skillful and respected ruler who had a favorable attitude toward the Jews in Palestine, even though he granted them no special privileges. Quirinius, on the other hand, was remembered by many Romans for meanness and exorbitant use of power late in his career. He seems to have been an unsavory character.

I also learned there are questions regarding the accuracy of Luke's dating of the first registration. Regardless of how these may be resolved, I noticed that an emperor with a favorable reputation among the Jews, and a lesser official with an unfavorable reputation among many Romans are named in Luke 2:1-2.

If nothing else, this emphasizes how *ordinary* life was on the day Christ was born. So ordinary that there are no clear historical records to confirm or disconfirm some of the items in Luke's opening verse! No one knew it was a momentous day for "all the world" (vv. 2:1, 10). People think they are being registered to be taxed. But in reality something bigger than any of them could imagine is happening as well.

God's work goes on not alongside but right in the middle of everyday transactions. So everyday they may not even be recorded or remembered by everyone. What's happening is for *everyone*. Even Augustus and Quirinius. The Jews and the Romans. Joseph and Mary. The shepherds and "all who heard it." *All* the people being registered that day, savory and unsavory, the travelers and the innkeeper. Maybe even the sheep!

When I finally realized I had gotten sidetracked from the process, I felt discouraged and frustrated. I had spent more time and energy on this part of the exercise than was necessary. I decided to work immediately on two or three details that stood out to me in the text. I hoped I could do this without consciously or explicitly tying them into what

I had just worked on in the Bible encyclopedia. I read the text again. The details that stood out were about Mary.

   —The contrast between Mary's response and the response of other people (to the shepherds) still hooked my interest. (vv. 18-19)

   —Luke has more than one description of Mary's situation and actions. (vv. 5-7, 19)

   —Luke names Mary before Joseph in 2:16.

Here's how these details helped me understand what's going on in the text. It seems Mary is almost lost in the commotion surrounding Jesus' birth. But Luke wants us to notice her, not just to assume her presence. Not only was the birth of Jesus not lost in the flow of everyday life, Mary wasn't either.

Today we would hardly expect Jesus' birth to be overlooked. But Mary is a different matter. How many mothers, whether they are considered successful or not, have been swallowed up in everyday events? Or disappeared entirely into the larger scene? Luke doesn't want this to happen to Mary.

It's no secret that Mary was in a less-than-ideal situation as a pregnant, unmarried mother. She seems caught up in events beyond her control. But Luke wants us to know what's going on with Mary. He wants us to know she isn't just amazed (like all the others) by the shepherds' report, but treasures all their words and ponders them in her heart.

For the next three days, I didn't work on the text. On the fourth day I checked in with myself before going on. We had moved my daughter during those three days, and on this fourth day I was sad, grieving, disoriented, confused, devastated, lonely, and caught up in emotions I couldn't even name. I unfairly took out some of my frustration on my husband by picking an argument about cat food. I attended a support group in the morning, but was afraid to share because I didn't want to start crying again. I talked with a close friend afterward and felt encouraged and hopeful. She knew what I was going through because she has been there, too.

I also reread all my notes before going on. This led to further insights which pointed me to other details in the text. The material below is taken directly from my notebook.

> I wonder. Maybe the angel and the angel choir were for *Mary's* benefit. Not just the shepherds'. Here the thing she was told about has come to pass, but how is she to know it wasn't all a dream? God sends messengers when she needs them—not always directly. The shepherds are an indirect angel choir for Mary's benefit. The shepherds' story is bounded by references to Mary—her condition, her activity, her response.

> I'm also thinking about Jesus, and how his ability to listen, and ponder what he heard, came from his mother. And perhaps too his sense of being chosen for a mission. Did she ever tell *her* story to Jesus?

> I think Mary's response is highlighted because, in some ways, Luke is presenting Mary's and not just Jesus' story. This is confirmed by connections to what goes before and after this passage. Actually, Luke is giving us the family picture—Zechariah and Elizabeth; then Mary and Elizabeth; then Zechariah, Elizabeth and John; and then Mary and Joseph and Jesus.

> Then Luke goes beyond the immediate family to the shepherds and Jesus; Simeon, Mary, Joseph, and Jesus; Anna and Jesus; Jesus and his parents with the travelers and teachers.

References to *Mary's responses*:
1:29 perplexed and pondered
2:19 treasured these words and pondered them
2:33 amazed
2:48 astonished and anxious
2:50 did not understand
2:51 treasured all these things

Things don't just *happen* in the Bible. They are part of the stuff of everyday attitudes, responses, feelings. Jesus didn't just come into the world in general. Jesus came into a very human set of circumstances that included complex emotions and responses—things that don't normally get thought of as "the data" to be recorded. Luke doesn't just highlight Mary's feelings. He also evokes emotions in his readers, and describes them in the shepherds, the angels, and all who heard the shepherd's witness.

Jesus is born into an everyday world of events. He is also born into an everyday world of feelings. The good news of great joy is for our hearts. Luke highlights feelings throughout. He evokes them, describes circumstances that suggest them.

What does it mean to think of the redemption of our feelings? Amazement pervades these two chapters. When God comes in human form, are we invited into amazement? I'm not sure. Fear pervades these chapters also. As does praise and gratitude. And wonder. And excitement. And peace. And perplexity. Astonishment. Anxiety. Longing. Joy. *Every* human emotion!

This is a real world. Not emotionless! Real, not just because of the decree from the emperor, but because the people being described aren't robots playing out a predetermined set of roles. This is just like our lives!

When I came to the end of Step Three, I didn't find anything I wished the text had said differently. I named the following things I was pretty sure the text didn't mean, and did mean.

> —This isn't just the story of Jesus' birth. It's also the story of Mary as his mother.
> —This isn't about the wonder of motherhood or about Mary the perfect mother. It's about Mary as a real, live human being who, like many of us mothers, didn't have the best start in life with her first child.
> —This isn't just the story of Jesus' birth. It's also the story of many different events surrounding it. Jesus isn't born into a vacuum, unconnected from the rest of life.
> —This isn't about Christmas as such, but about how God comes to the real world of events and people, great and small, seemingly significant and seemingly insignificant.

Finally I described how I saw this story as the story of my life.

> I'm very caught up right now in a real world of family events, very aware of my role as a mother. There is great comfort for me in seeing how God cares for Mary in these chapters. She's in a very unenviable position. But God doesn't abandon her. God sends messengers, directly and indirectly, to let her know that God hasn't abandoned her, or left her without any neighbors who also are tuned in to what God is doing in their world.
> Mary must have been confused and unsure about what would happen to her and to her child. I identify strongly with those dynamics. And I'm invited by this

text to expect messengers from God, to keep my eyes open, especially to the everyday things in which I least expect to hear God's messengers.

Step Four: Thinking about hiding

It wasn't difficult to see how I've hidden from this text. I've *distanced* it by reading it as a record of certain events, without acknowledging the human emotions described by Luke as part of the events. They aren't secondary or merely descriptive. They are part of the real world of the people in Luke 1 and 2.

I tend to overlook their feelings because I tend to overlook my own. Even though I have many feelings in the course of a day, I tend to highlight only some. I acknowledge those I'm most comfortable with, or those I think define my day (whether they do or not). I grew up being warned against being ruled by my feelings. I've been afraid to own my feelings. But here I see that Mary's feelings are a crucial part of her story and of her relationship to her son. They aren't an unwelcome, embarrassing intrusion. They are part of *life*.

I stopped at this point. When I continued the following evening, I first did a quick inventory of my feelings. I was frustrated and discouraged because one of my writing projects was turning out to be more difficult than I had anticipated. I had just finished rewriting a section I'd struggled with for a week. I was relieved to have it done, but knew I had another section to go. Also I had just remembered an invitation to which I had forgotten to respond on time. The beginning of the school year was close, and I felt unprepared.

I had done a few things to take care of myself that day, and realized I was doing better than I thought. Nonetheless, I felt panic about the next several weeks, and regret that I hadn't accomplished everything I had set out to do over the summer. That week had been especially difficult. My emotions were like a whirlwind, not calm at all.

I looked back over my first responses to the text. I could see something that was right. The text *is* about the real world. But I hadn't yet seen that the text was connected to the real world of human emotions, hopes, and fears. It seemed to be mainly about certain events that surrounded the birth of Jesus. I hadn't noticed the human emotions Luke had carefully included in his account.

Step Five: Taking another look

Though I didn't find this passage enemy-like on the days I worked on it, I did find my interpretation of it disturbing. Here's a summary of what I wrote.

I know from experience that human emotions are sometimes belittled, scoffed at, and overlooked. Sometimes people would rather deal with concepts, ideas, data, or hard evidence. But I hear this text as good news about human emotions. Not just that they're allowed, but that they are part of God's good creation as well as part of God's redemptive *re*-creation. In this text they let me know these people weren't robots and weren't living in some spiritual realm "above it all." Their emotions are part of their story.

I'm not entirely comfortable with this way of interpreting the text because I'm not entirely comfortable with all of my emotions these days. I like to be in control of my feelings, but I seem to be out of control and overwhelmed by some of them, especially sadness and anxiety.

This story is about God bringing peace into the world. I would like to know peace in relation to my feelings. Not so I don't have them, but so I accept them as a part of who I am. They are as much a channel of God's grace to me, and of my sharing that grace, as are my thoughts and ideas. I would like to be liberated in my emotions. I still war against them, trying to deny or trivialize them, instead of accepting them as part of my connection to God and to other people.

Jonah 1 and 2

(from Elouise's journal)

Step One: Getting in touch with myself

As I began working on this text I was struggling to stay connected to what was going on in my life on that day. I knew I was responsible just for that day, but my mind kept racing ahead, dragging my feelings with it. It was my daughter's first day of classes, and I kept wondering how she was doing. I had just phoned a friend to respond late to a dinner invitation. She was kind, much kinder than I had been to myself about responding late. I was aware of my urge to procrastinate, and I had an important project I wanted to complete that day even though I had done next to nothing on it so far.

A close friend had called the day before to tell me her best friend had just died. I hadn't known this person was her best friend, so the intensity of her disbelief and shock was unexpected. I wasn't sure how to respond. I decided to listen and be as supportive as I could. I felt helpless and unsure of myself.

I was also thinking about my professional identity, about which I had felt unsettled for a while. It was time to clarify my long-term goals and take action to begin moving in certain directions. I was afraid to be too clear, though, because it would mean changing some comfortable routines I had gotten into on my job. I knew it was time for change, but I felt anxious about the outcome.

I decided to work on Jonah 1 and 2, even though it's rather long. I wanted to include the part about the fish. I've *always* heard this as a story about obeying God and about what a mess you'll get yourself into if you try to run away from what God wants you to do. And sometimes the thing God wants you to do has been presented as calling down judgment on sinners, or going where you least want to go, doing what you least want to do. I'm supposed to be wiser than Jonah and follow God's will for my life.

I remembered a children's song that made an impression on me. I still remember all the words, and wrote them in my notes.

> God sent Jonah on an errand, but Jonah disobeyed.
> He hid by going to the bottom of a ship,
> And there he stayed.
> While at sea a big storm came;
> And Jonah knew he was to blame.
> They threw Jonah in the sea;
> A big whale swallowed him in-stant-ly!
> In the whale he was so sad;
> He was sorry for being bad.
> God forgave him once more;
> And the whale threw Jonah on the shore!

Here are things that stood out the first time I read through Jonah 1 and 2.

—"Jonah set out to flee to Tarshish from the presence of the Lord" (1:3)

—"away from the presence of the Lord" (1:3)

—"fleeing from the presence of the Lord" (1:10)

—contrasting themes throughout: Jonah *fleeing* from the presence of the Lord, and the persistent *presence* of the Lord

—the sailors (1:11-16)

—Jonah says the *Lord* cast him into the deep (2:3)

—Jonah's repentance seems to be the result of God wielding a bigger stick than Jonah (chapter 2)

—Jonah's words, "what I have vowed I will pay" (2:9)

Avoidance. This was the first connection I made between what I saw in the text and what I saw going on in my life. Jonah attempted to flee from the presence of the Lord; I have procrastinated to avoid work I know I must do this fall.

However, the main connection was with professional identity. God called Jonah to do something he apparently didn't want to do. It involved taking a stand against Nineveh's wickedness. Jonah didn't seem thrilled about this. I had been thinking about my professional identity in the twenty-four-hours before I worked on the text. I still wasn't sure what stands I might need to take to accomplish things God had called me to do.

I don't like taking stands, especially when they might be dangerous to my professional health. It's easy to identify with Jonah's desire to flee rather than taking a stand in an uncertain situation. Jonah seems very human in his response. I understand his desire to lie down and go to sleep.

One other connection stood out. I had just responded late to a dinner invitation. The woman to whom I talked was kind. Jonah responded late to God's "invitation" (2:9). God gave Jonah another opportunity to respond (3:1).

I had fears about God and fears about myself in relation to this text. I was afraid it would be about God using a big stick to get us to repent and be obedient children. God would be an angry, controlling, demanding God. Kind and merciful only when we're obedient. Raging at us the rest of the time, making life difficult so we'll knuckle under.

As for myself, I sometimes fear that I'm on the wrong road. I fear I'm doing what *I* want to do instead of what *God* wants me to do. Maybe I'm Jonah, trying to run away from the Lord. Maybe I don't even know how I'm doing this, and won't, until I'm down and out in the belly of a fish. Maybe my childhood impressions about this story will turn out to be right. I've disobeyed God, and I'm to blame when things around me go badly.

By the time I returned to the text the following day, I had been twenty minutes late for an important appointment. This fit a pattern of lateness over the last few days. I felt devastated as I drove to the appointment, and fought the urge to punish myself verbally.

Other things also weighed me down during that twenty-four-hour period. I wasn't looking forward to the beginning of the school year. The national election campaign was feeling particularly ugly toward women. I felt alone and isolated. My body was registering stress and anxiety. I had changed my calendar to a new month and had been reminded of many little things I hadn't done yet. I felt overwhelmed. I tried to reach my daughter on the phone, but she wasn't in. I was disappointed and sad when I went to bed.

Step Two: Accepting my limitations

I had already decided to spend one to one and a half hours a day on the text. I spent five days working on it, spread over eight days.

Here's what I didn't understand in Jonah 1 and 2.

—In 1:3 Jonah sets out to flee. *Why?* And is this

bad? I've always assumed it was. Also, Jonah seems to think he can flee the presence of the Lord by going to Tarshish. But isn't the Lord in Tarshish?

—I've always assumed 1:4 was about the Lord punishing Jonah. But what's really going on here? Also, I've always assumed the Lord didn't respect Jonah's choice to flee. Is this what's going on? I'm not sure.

—In 1:11 the sailors don't obey Jonah immediately, even though they fear for their lives. What does this mean, and why is it important to the story?

—In 2:1 Jonah prays to the Lord. This seems to be the first time Jonah speaks directly to the Lord. Is this significant? If so, how?

—In 2:2 Jonah refers to his distress and to the Lord answering him. I'm not sure when and where all this takes place. I've always assumed Jonah was referring to his distress in the belly of the fish, and to the Lord's response to that particular situation. But could his distress and the Lord's answer refer to other times and places in the story as well?

—The prayer that begins in 2:2 seems more like a report of a prayer, and the Lord's response to it, than a prayer itself. Is this significant? If so, why?

I had already decided to stay with *The International Standard Bible Encyclopedia (ISBE)* for this exercise.

Step Three: Accepting the Bible just as it is

I decided to look at several things: *details* in the text, the *form* of the text, the *situation* depicted in the text, and *connections* between the first two chapters and the rest of the book.

I began with a detail that pointed to part of the situation. Tarshish is mentioned three times in the first three verses, while Nineveh is mentioned only once. It seemed important to understand Tarshish, not just Nineveh.

Again I didn't pay attention to instructions and went immediately to *ISBE*. Before long I was bogged down in details that didn't seem helpful. I was losing my focus on the text itself. I realized what I had done, and got back on track. I also realized that sometimes I would rather have others tell me how they would answer a question of interpretation, than spend time with the text figuring out how I might answer the same question. It isn't a matter of not wanting to be in conversation with other interpreters. It's a matter of hoping they'll answer my questions for me, so I won't need to spend time figuring out what I think is going on in the text.

I got back to the text itself and looked for details the narrator had given about Tarshish and Nineveh in 1:1-3. Here's what I found.

—Nineveh is named first. It is "that great city" known to God for its wickedness and in need of immediate aid (Jonah is told to "Go at once.").

—Tarshish isn't described directly. It is clearly *not* on the way to Nineveh and must be reached by ship. Jonah thinks he will get away from the Lord's presence by fleeing to Tarshish. The narrator names Tarshish three times.

I decided the narrator's threefold naming of Tarshish might be a way of underscoring Jonah's determination not to go to Nineveh. Jonah didn't just turn a deaf ear to God's command. Rather, he firmly fixed in his mind a different destination and set out to do whatever it took to get there (1:3). Also, this emphatic naming of Tarshish along with Nineveh suggests these are real places, not just symbols of some spiritual reality. The story is about a real human being in the real world.

Next I listed several *contrasts* I had seen in chapters 1 and 2.

—Jonah slept, while the sailors struggled to survive.

—Chapter 1 is filled with action-packed dialogue and narrative. Chapter 2 is in the form of a poetic prayer (that nonetheless contains reported dialogue and narrative).

—For the sailors, the storm ended when they picked Jonah up and threw him into the sea. For Jonah, the storm seemed to begin as he hit the water.

—Jonah's main activity in chapter 1 is fleeing. His main activity in chapter 2 is praying.

—In chapter 1 the sailors cry out to their gods. Even though Jonah is told to call on his God, he does not.

The next day I spent several minutes checking in before I continued. It was the first day of the fall semester, the day I would meet new students. I was nervous about this. I was also frustrated because some books I needed were at my office. I felt sad that summer vacation was ending. I had read some disturbing magazine articles the night before and wasn't sure why these peoples' stories had affected me so strongly.

I reviewed all my notes and discovered yet another contrast. On the one hand, the theme of chapter 1 is Jonah fleeing from the presence of the Lord. On the other hand, the theme of chapter 1 is also the Lord's presence everywhere around Jonah, even in the storm.

I wasn't sure what to make of the contrasts I had seen. Some of them heightened the irrationality of Jonah's actions. It's absurd that he thinks he can flee the presence of the Lord, that he goes to sleep, and that he doesn't pray to the Lord. At least it *seems* absurd. I already know the story. Jonah didn't. Maybe it didn't seem absurd to him.

I've always assumed Jonah was stubborn and pigheaded, that he just didn't want or like this assignment. But looking at it again, who *wouldn't* run from this? It's as though God were telling Jonah to go and commit professional suicide. It just doesn't make sense from the human point of view. If God's command doesn't make sense (sending one obviously reluctant person against "that great city Nineveh" with no promise of other prophets to share the task), then Jonah's actions made *great* sense. They make sense even though we're not told yet why he flees. He just wants to be out of the presence of the Lord—*this* Lord, who gave him *this* task!

I turned next to the *form* of the text, especially the contrasting poetic prayer of chapter 2. Poetry conveys feelings and emotions. This poetry, in the form of a psalm, is presented as a prayer. But it isn't just a prayer. It's a rehearsal, in poetic form, of what happened inside *Jonah*. It's as though we're finally being given a chance to see what's going on inside this man who *seems* blatantly unfeeling and uncaring, even about his own life.

The poem is set in the belly of the fish, but I wonder whether Jonah's distress (2:2) began long before he found himself in the belly of the fish. The prayer seems as much about his inner turmoil about the word of the Lord as it is about being in the belly of the fish. In any case, his external situation seems to reflect accurately his internal struggle to decide whether to heed the word of the Lord. This all reconfirms the awesome, fearsome nature of the task—*not* that there is anything wrong about Jonah.

A *detail* seemed important at this point. In 2:3 Jonah says, "You [the Lord] cast me into the deep. . . ." In 2:4 he describes himself being driven away from the sight of the Lord. This seems significant because in chapter 1 the sailors cast Jonah into the sea, and Jonah is actively choosing to flee from the presence of the Lord. Perhaps this means God honored Jonah's desire to flee. Perhaps God gave Jonah what he was seeking but didn't abandon him in the process (1:17; 2:6, 10).

Yet another *detail* caught my attention. In 1:4 the narrator says, *"But* [emphasis mine] the Lord hurled a great wind upon the sea. . . ."* I've always assumed that meant God set out to punish Jonah immediately, acting in direct opposition to Jonah's flight. But there may be another way of hearing this. Jonah apparently thought that by going to Tarshish he would flee the presence of the Lord (1:4). The Lord, on the other hand, sets out to grant his desire before he gets to Tarshish. This would mean that even the setting in which Jonah feels cut off from God's presence (2:4) is clearly in God's hands.

Does this mean God is manipulating Jonah? No, because even in Tarshish (or Nineveh) the narrator hints that the Lord will be present. The Lord is clearly following this ship going to Tarshish. Also, according to Jonah's own witness (1:9) the Lord made the sea and the dry land. The story suggests that fleeing from the presence of this Lord is something *we* try to do, even against what we say we believe.

In the whale Jonah felt driven from the sight of the Lord (2:4), but the Lord still heard his prayer (2:7). Perhaps the Lord is granting Jonah's desire, but in a way that confirms the Lord's presence.

I looked next at *connections* between the first two chapters and the rest of the story. Right away (3:1) I saw that God gave Jonah a second chance. I also saw that in the meantime God had given Jonah time to reflect on the first command. The rest of the story sheds light on why this task was so awesome. It wasn't because Jonah might fail and get kicked out of the city, but because he might succeed—and be unhappy with God's decision not to destroy repentant, believing Nineveh.

The rest of the story also let me know Jonah and God weren't strangers. Jonah knew God well, and there were things about God that Jonah didn't like. He didn't like what God was famous for—"a gracious God and merciful, slow to anger, and abounding in steadfast love, and ready to relent from punishing" (4:2). Yet precisely *this* God also saved Jonah's life, something God sets out to make clear to Jonah (4:6-11). Jonah doesn't have the heart of the Creator (4:11 and 1:9). He has the heart of a human being. Looking back, I could see that God cares as much for Jonah's life as for the inhabitants of Nineveh.

I didn't work on the text for two days. On the third day I took a few minutes to check in with myself. I was feeling better than I had for about a week. I had just returned from a workout. I had also been to a dinner party the night before and had split my sides laughing and sharing with good friends.

At the same time, I felt a little like an outsider, since I don't move in the same informal circles as some of these friends, or share common memories of the music and dances of the 1950s. I was there in the '50s, but I wasn't part of the teenage scene. Nor did I have stories from the present to somehow make up for it. So my enjoyment of the evening felt spectator-like, and I knew that beneath my laughter was pain, jealousy, and an edge of self-pity. I felt awkward and embarrassed, like an insider who couldn't change the reality of also being an outsider.

I reviewed my notes, and identified two questions I hadn't addressed yet from Step Two.

—Is it significant that Jonah doesn't speak directly to the Lord until 2:1?

—Why is it important that the sailors don't obey Jonah immediately, even though they were in dire circumstances? (1:11-15)

I answered the second question first. It occurred to me that the sailors showed more concern for the life of this one human being than Jonah did for all the human beings and animals of Nineveh. The sailors didn't even know

Jonah's God, the Creator. Yet their hearts seem to be closer to the Creator's heart in that moment than Jonah's is. They didn't want to be guilty of sending this one human being to his death. Perhaps the narrator is inviting me to contrast this with Jonah's response to the Ninevites, who were also in danger of perishing.

The other question was about Jonah's prayer. In 2:1, the narrator says, "*Then* [emphasis mine] Jonah prayed to the Lord his God. . . ." When? After being in the belly of the fish three days and three nights. It seems Jonah didn't want to have anything to do with the Lord his God, even though he says in 1:9 that he worships this God. According to the narrator, Jonah didn't pray in chapter 1. Weren't things yet bad enough? Obviously they were. The sailors prayed to their gods (1:5), and the captain urged Jonah to pray to his god (1:6).

The prayer of Jonah seems to parallel the prayers of the Ninevites. They, too, cried out to God because they were in danger of perishing. Perhaps this parallelism is another way of underscoring Jonah's humanity. The narrator doesn't put the prophet on a level above everyone else. He is himself in need of God's deliverance, just like the sailors and the Ninevites. At the same time, look at what Jonah went through before he prayed! There's a parallel with the Ninevites, but there's also a contrast. The Ninevites, who presumably don't know this God, seem more willing to heed God than does Jonah, who knows God well. Even the fish obeys God more readily than does Jonah (1:17 and 2:10)! No wonder God's heart has room for animals (4:11).

When I came to the end of Step Three I didn't find anything on that day that I wished the text said differently. Here's what I was pretty sure the text is and isn't about.

—It isn't primarily about judgment, or about Jonah being disobedient. Instead, it's primarily about the Lord's presence, grace, persistence, patience, and care for creation (especially children and animals, 4:11).

—It isn't about God forcing Jonah to do it God's way. Rather, it's about God working through a human being who preferred, even to the end, to have things *his* way.

—It isn't about God as angry, controlling, or demanding. Rather, it's about God's kindness and mercy even when Jonah was difficult and uncooperative. It's also about Jonah's harsh judgment of God, and Jonah's anger toward God for being merciful, slow to anger, and ready to relent from punishing.

—It isn't about a superficially obedient robot. It's about a human being, and his anguished conflict over the word of the Lord that came to him.

Finally I tried to connect the story of Jonah with what was going on in my life. At first I didn't see a specific connection. I didn't have a word to cry out against Nineveh, though I *do* have a word to cry out against wickedness. Also, I didn't think of myself as a prophet like Jonah.

But then I made a deeper connection. I was certain about this: *God won't forsake me*, even if I consciously set out to flee from God's presence. God didn't forsake the sailors, Jonah, or the Ninevites. I, too, am God's creature. I don't need to wonder whether each step I'm taking in these difficult days is precisely the "right" step. God will let me know when I try to flee. I can trust God for this, just as much as I can trust God for my salvation.

Later that day I saw another connection. I'm like Jonah. I flee from the presence of the Lord because I would rather not experience God's mercy and love. I would rather pass judgment on myself and others than accept God's care and concern. I see this clearly in my need to dwell on how much I've procrastinated, and in how awful I felt about being late. I would rather pass harsh judgment on myself, and punish myself, than accept myself as I am. I also see this in my tendency, when describing what's going on in my life, to focus on the negative. I flee from God's loving, merciful presence.

Jonah wasn't running from God's harshness (4:2). He was running from God's love for Nineveh and for Jonah himself. He did this by putting himself in a position he knew didn't reflect the truth about himself as a Hebrew, or about the God he worshiped (1:9). He set himself up to experience the absence of God's love.

I do this too. The truth is that God is *still* present, and loves me anyway. So I might as well stop wasting negative time and energy avoiding God's mercy. The task didn't overwhelm Jonah (3:3-5); God's mercy did (4:1)!

Step Four: Thinking about hiding

As I looked back over my notes I could hear that I *distance* this text. I have difficulty identifying with Jonah. I don't like to think I'm fleeing from the presence of the Lord. I pray every day and think about God a lot. My job requires it!

My initial understanding of this text focused on what Jonah was called to *do* in Nineveh. This was a safe focus, since I feel I'm in the right job at the present. I didn't yet see that Jonah was being called to live with God's mercy, to experience it for himself, and only then to proclaim it to people he considered his enemies.

My initial understanding was right because Jonah *did* encounter God's mercy in Nineveh, a foreign land. It was important to go to Nineveh, but not to call down the wrath of God on that city. Rather, only in Nineveh did Jonah's real reason for fleeing the presence of the Lord become visible, so that he came face to face with *his* desire for judgment to fall on Nineveh.

Two days later I saw something else in this story. When God first called Jonah to go to Nineveh, Jonah wasn't ready for the task. Not because he didn't know what to say to the Ninevites, but because he didn't yet have a sense of God's mercy for *him.*

Ironically, when Jonah finally reaches Nineveh, he demonstrates that he still isn't in touch with God's mercy—even though he's proclaiming it throughout the city. God patiently prepares yet another learning session for Jonah. First a bush, then an east wind. And Jonah still behaves like a human being full of self-destructive feelings and behaviors.

I know what this is like. I read about Jonah and determine that I will be different. I'll get the lesson straight the first time. But I don't. The message is simple enough: God cares deeply not just for all creation—but for me. Getting ready for the work to which God calls me means experiencing in my life what I say I believe, God's mercy toward me. How strange that this is precisely what I fear most. Maybe I know it means God is also merciful toward those I consider to be my enemies.

Step Five: Taking another look

As I reread Jonah 1 and 2, I still didn't like the part about God hurling a great wind upon the sea (1:4). I find it frightening. It still sounds like harsh punishment, even though there is no indication in the text that God is out to punish or destroy Jonah. In fact, the entire narrative suggests God wants to get close to Jonah as his deliverer. Yet this doesn't seem to be the act of a merciful God. Why didn't God engage Jonah in a discussion? Or take some less drastic measure?

I decided the text might be inviting me to keep an open mind about God. Perhaps I am to trust that *God* knows what it will take to get Jonah's attention while still respecting Jonah's desire to flee.

In the same way, perhaps I'm to keep an open mind about things that suddenly come into my life. Perhaps I, too, am fleeing from the presence of a merciful God, and only God knows what it will take to get my attention. I'm tempted to view these storms as punishment, whether I expect them or not. But perhaps God wants to invite me, in the midst of the storm, to remember God's mercy.

I know that my own experience of childhood punishment affects the way I hear this story. When I was young, intervention by higher human authorities supposedly meant I was being bad, and that some balancing of the moral scales was in order. I had to *pay* somehow for my disobedience, as part of setting things right.

But God isn't a human parent. Sometimes fleeing from human authority figures is a survival tactic. Human authority figures don't always have my best interests at heart, even though they're convinced they do. Fleeing from God is an entirely different matter. It is *not* a survival tactic, as Jonah discovered.

At the same time, I know how easy it is to flee from God's mercy, especially when accepting God's mercy means I might have to change my mind about myself or about my enemies. Sometimes it seems I would rather die than switch.

Romans 8:1-18

(from Louis's journal)

Step One: Getting in touch with myself

March 8. 4:00 p.m. It is late afternoon. I am finally getting to work on this text after feeling like a failure for several days. I have just recently had a conversation with a co-worker about things that had become confusing between us, and I am feeling relieved that our relationship is clear and positive.

I have a growing sense of making progress on some personal issues, but I am haunted by feelings that nothing really changes. I have received some good news recently about some performance tests I have taken, but I am bothered by a gnawing concern about my income taxes; I don't have enough money to pay what is due!

4:15 p.m. I am selecting Romans 8 (New Revised Standard Version). I know it has a familiar phrase about condemnation and it is part of one of the letters in the New Testament. It will make a good model for reading something other than a story with our method. I am going to focus on verses 1-18, just because it seems like a good place to stop. A new paragraph begins in verse 19, and there sure seems to be enough stuff in the first 18 verses.

How have I heard this text in the past? I have always liked this text. I have remembered the opening phrase, "There is therefore now no condemnation. . . ." That has always been good news to me. I fear condemnation and want to believe it is never helpful. I know this text is part of a letter that Paul wrote to a group of Christians. I anticipate the meaning will be hard to grasp; I've always felt that Paul's words were too big for me.

What jumps out at me today:
>—no condemnation
>—God has done what before was thought not done
>—to set the mind on the Spirit is life and peace
>—If the Spirit of him who raised Jesus from the dead dwells in you, the one who raised Christ from the dead will give life to your mortal bodies also
>—children of God . . . no spirit of slavery . . . no falling back into fears!

4:30 p.m. What are the connections? An issue that drives me away from personal interaction with colleagues is fear of condemnation.

April 26. 10:45 p.m. A day for myself. I feel like reading. The following paragraphs continue the search for connections and name my fears about this text.

It has been a long time since I looked at this text. I have carried it with me over one and a half months. As I reread what I wrote about this text, I realize that the same phrase I said I like the most is also the phrase I like the least.

My thoughts go like this. If there is "no condemnation," why do I feel it so much? I feel condemned a lot. Even about letting so much time go by since I last worked on this passage. In the month and a half of carrying the text with me, remembering it as I sat at red lights and as I got ready to go to bed, during days when I remembered it on purpose and times it surprised me, I often felt condemned. By voices that go beyond my sense of control.

Perhaps this is what Paul means when he says that he struggles with setting his mind on "the flesh"—the mind set on the flesh is hostile to God. When I hear the words "no condemnation," I hear hostile voices saying it isn't really so!

I've lived with this one a *while*—and it sometimes describes a life that I rarely know! Verse 15 says that you did not receive the spirit of slavery—to fall back into fear! But you have received the spirit of "sonship." What grand words! They point to a way of life I have only glimpsed. Paul seems to be appealing to the part of me that longs for acceptance and for freedom. It makes me wonder—where does condemnation come from?

I really like being a child of God. It is a happy thought! I have a fantasy of what that is like. Freedom to make mistakes, to grow, to be ignorant of some things, to cry *Abba*—Daddy—to God and expect a loving and fair response. I don't know what this is like in real life. I almost thought about writing some things about my own dad, and then I remembered he might read this, and so probably will my son and my daughters.

I feel like crying as I think about how little I really know about how to give or receive love that doesn't condemn. But the words of Paul are wonderful. No condemning, living in the Spirit of God, life and peace, to be led by the Spirit of God. I hear Paul making room for persons who are not "living in the Spirit"—the spirit of Christ is not in them. Maybe that's it. Maybe in this text I have found the handle to be free to condemn myself. I'm one of those that the spirit of Christ doesn't dwell in.

So this text raises a question that always pops up when

I read such descriptions of life with God. Am I in the group? I really don't like this part of my inner life. I always want someone or something to assure me that I am one of the group of people that these promises are meant for. I am nearly forty years old and I've had this discussion going on for most of those years.

I also hear the connections to my inner struggles with my co-workers. I need to fear condemnation. I carry the expectation of it wherever I go, and so I am greatly relieved when it doesn't happen!

Step Two: Accepting my limitations

April 26. 11:35 a.m. I have one hour to work on this passage today. I will attempt to spend at least one hour at each work session so that I can keep continuity. My schedule is busy and I don't know what kind of regular time I will give this. I want to complete the total project with about six hours of time spent. That may take a while.

Many things are unclear to me. I do not understand any of these words: justification, reckoned, flesh, likeness of sinful flesh, walking according to the Spirit, dwell, according to the flesh, and (mostly) condemnation. These phrases create feelings of inadequacy in me. I read the first words and they say there is no condemnation, but I feel condemned in the face of my lack of understanding. What is Paul addressing here—the same issues running in my head?

My main resource for understanding this part will be *Romans*, a commentary by James G. Dunn I have in my library. I will use my dictionary to look up the meanings of the English words that I don't use and try to get a clearer understanding.

I used most of my time on this passage just trying to read and understand the English translation. It is now 2:40 p.m.

Step Three: Accepting the Bible just as it is

2:45 p.m. Two or three *details* stand out. Condemnation. This one just keeps coming up as a theme underlying the whole section. What is condemnation? Where does it come from and what is Paul saying about it?

Another phrase that stands out is "living in the flesh." I wonder what this looks like today?

What does it mean to be a child of God, and how does that help with condemnation? This whole section seems to be an argument such as a trial lawyer would present before a judge.

The *form* of the text is a letter. It is written to people the author assumes are sympathetic to his cause, but they need more information.

The *writer* of the text is named as Paul. I know that this Paul was very educated, but he had been through some big changes in his life. I know that in his past he had been a very zealous person, forcing others to obey the law.

The text is written sometime after the death of Jesus, but recently enough that Paul uses that death and the resurrection as a basis for proof of what he has to say about how to live now. I think this is important because I realize that to understand the intensity of his concern I have to hear how sure he was about Jesus and who Jesus was.

My attention is fading as I try to read the passages before and after my chosen section. The argument seems terse and unconnected. I am going to let it rest until tomorrow.

April 27. 10:15 a.m. I reread the text today and realize that while it may be true that there is no condemnation for those in Christ, there is condemnation for me. Perhaps not from God, but from me. I can find five things in any moment of the day for which I could easily be condemned. This is the thing that keeps coming back to me that I want to work on. So I struggle onward looking at the context and reading what comes before and after, trying to get a handle on what Paul is saying.

In verse 18, the part that comes after this, I notice that Paul talks about the meaning of suffering. That lets me know that part of what Paul is discussing here is a source of suffering. I am still wondering about this flesh thing. Why does Paul have to tell me that I am not in it? Why such a neatly arranged argument? It reads like a manuscript for a trial, and Paul seems to be offering a defense. In the previous part he talks about being a slave to two masters at the same time. One master is the Law of God which gives life, and the other master is the law of sin which brings death.

Now I am beginning to hear a context for some of these big words. The trial or struggle describes a conflict within Paul and me and every other human who tries to follow God. The struggle is within us as well as a part of just living in this world.

As part of the discussion, Paul refers to Abraham's faith. I remember the struggle Abraham had in holding on until Sarah gave birth to his first child. God had promised a lot of descendants, yet as Abraham and Sarah headed ever closer to the century mark, descendants had yet to arrive!

This story and Paul's use of it raises the image of being suspended between two realities. On the one hand we have the life promised by God and hoped for by humans. On the other hand we have the present moment which seems to point to a failure on God's part.

Paul seems to forget that in his moment of trial Abraham caved in and had a child by another woman. Was this by deception? But in Paul's mind Abraham is still an example of how God accomplishes things with those who continue to trust.

The text is beginning to make more sense now. But I

think I need to hear the whole discussion. I am going to read the whole letter up to this point. It is only six pages. I will try to read it in ten minutes. I am still working on the same list from Step Two. After I have read the whole six pages I am going to look at the resources.

Reading notes: Our injustice serves to confirm the justice of *God*. I don't understand how this works. We are justified by God's grace/faith? (I feel like engaging the author in a dialogue.) God, the one who justifies the ungodly—trusting, without works. . . . Righteousness reckoned to them. . . . I need to know what "reckoning" means, so I'll look it up in my dictionary. Reckoning—paid to the account of. A term used in financial arrangements. Paul says God has paid these things to our account.

> —Life to the dead (the powerless). In this case our sense of powerlessness is compared to being dead.
> —Calls into existence things that do not exist!
> —Hope against hope.

Each of these is impossible without *God*! No one but God can "reckon" these things to us. And we need all three. When Abraham considered the possibility of having children with Sarah at their late age, he could have given up! But Paul says he did not weaken in faith when he considered his own body.

This is what happens to me! I weaken in faith when I consider *my* body. This is a good description of what I have been writing about. I feel empowered in my faith—just from reading that when Abraham considered his own body, which "was already as good as dead," he did not waver in his trust in God! Instead he grew strong in his faith.

This discovery alone makes me want to just stop and drink the power of it. The images Paul uses in the letter are directed to my struggle. The death of Jesus is a powerful image of where I am in relation to God. I am dead, but . . . I can hear Paul say God raised Jesus from the dead! I said earlier I wanted a dialogue with Paul. Now I hear his voice.

"You must consider yourself dead to sin, and alive to God."

"Sin has no dominion over *you*."

"Present yourselves to your master! Which master do we present ourselves to? Present yourselves as slaves of righteousness."

Paul appeals to me to receive not wages, as if I had earned these things that I need, but to receive them as a gift.

"For I delight in the Law of God in my innermost self."

"But I am at war!"

Now I am hooked. The language has engaged my struggle. Paul's argument is convincing, not just about what I need, but about what the struggle is like for me.

11:45. Ten minutes turned into forty-five. Reading the text felt like a reading of my own mind! The struggle within, finding words to describe it, images of slavery, power-lessness, and yet power to present myself to a different slave owner. All this to describe the inner struggle to receive the good news that God takes the things that are dead and makes them alive.

I feel normal. My struggle, as hard as it is, is human.

Commentary notes—I want to use James D. G. Dunn's commentary on Romans 1-8. But I'm running out of time. I'm excited by the discovery that I've made by rereading—carefully. I want to hold on to what I've discovered. So I'm going on.

What *doesn't* the text mean? It doesn't mean that we are free to do whatever we want; it means that we are free, no matter what, to present ourselves to be instruments for life. It also doesn't mean that God does all the work for us in life. It isn't about laziness or encouraging us to despair.

The text is about the inner struggle and the outward

life. It describes this struggle using the imagery of slavery, feelings of comparing our felt powerlessness and the power of God. It describes how left to ourselves and our thoughts, we will always understand and believe ourselves to be victims of forces much bigger than our choices.

But in the middle of our self-pity and feelings of shame, Paul names our power to act, which comes from *trust*. Trusting that God is able to turn anything around as we begin to offer our choices to a new master. This is the pathway to life, and a marvelous description of my inner world and its connection to my life.

Step Four: Thinking about hiding

Reading this text isn't going to mean the end of my struggle for self-acceptance.

My initial impression was that Paul's words are too hard to grasp. A kind of distancing of Paul. His ways aren't like mine! Now I have a better sense of our common struggle. I'm still thinking that I've settled for only a small piece of the pie. But I also don't want to lose it, so I'm going to live with this piece. Trusting in God.

When I read this text in the beginning, my need to condemn myself was out of control. And so even though the text comes from one (I see now) struggling with that very issue, it seemed at first and for a long time like bad news. I just wanted to hide from it. I didn't read it for almost two months. I didn't need any help in putting myself down. So for almost two months the struggle Paul was having, and his discovery, seemed not to be helpful.

I'm also amazed that just by *reading* the first part of the letter, most of the need to lay it down disappeared. I feel funny not needing to turn to the commentary to gain these insights. I'm sure there are some good insights there, but I am excited with what has happened.

Step Five: Taking another look

Things I don't like about the text?

I don't like the way things are always either/or. Sin and goodness. I don't like words like "righteousness" or "flesh" that are so foreign to my life. I don't like having to read for forty-five minutes just to understand one part of what is meant. Wasn't there an easier way to describe this?

I also don't think being a slave to God is a good image. Why must I be a slave at all? What about freedom?

I worry that Paul is encouraging in me a kind of spiritual dividedness. This sounds like just ignoring our behavior and pretending everything will work out! It's not helpful to separate the body and the self like he seems to do.

I think these things bother me because I am always seeing things as good or bad. I'm working to accept my body as good, and to realize that sometimes my free-wheeling and whimsical spirit gets me into trouble, too. I'm trying to integrate. Paul is pulling things apart to explain, and I would just as soon ignore the whole thing.

I have a good guy-bad guy motif in my life. If I could just be only the good guy, then I would be fine. Some of this text feeds into my need to deny the spontaneous, the irresponsible, and the childlike side of who I continue to be.

Even as I write this, I am hearing the dialogue with Paul. He, too, is inviting me to accept all of who I am. The force of this discovery is strong in the words, "There is therefore now no condemnation." But I am not a slave to anything or anyone, except the one who calls me to life.

On the one hand, I didn't like the things that in the beginning I thought condemned me. For example, when Paul says "to those who are in Christ," I heard him making room to say, "Now this doesn't apply to everyone, only to those who fit in—only to club members." But in rereading the first seven chapters, I am overwhelmed by how hard

Paul works to name everyone as those who have received the gift of Jesus. I would have put this text away in favor of another more readable, accepting text.

Now those nuances seem irrelevant. The purpose is to defeat the power, sin and condemnation. This is what I usually tell myself I am looking for, but at first it appears as the opposite!

I think about how hard I work to be an accepting parent, friend, and spouse. Usually when left to myself, I arrive at a place of harsh judgment, nonacceptance, and condemnation. The answer to the words of Paul, "Who will deliver me?" as I understand them right now, seems to be Jesus! The risen Christ.

How can I be an accepting co-worker without the power of acceptance that comes from the good news of God's total acceptance of *me*?

Epilogue

Making Friends with the Bible invites you to begin recognizing your patterns of hiding from the Bible and replacing them with patterns of friendship. It describes a process for putting friendship with the Bible into practice and shows what the process looks like.

Now it's up to you.

You may be wondering whether it's necessary to go through all the steps and exercises. Perhaps it seems a bit obsessive and highly structured, even artificial.

Making friends with the Bible isn't dependent on this or any other process. There's nothing magical about it. The steps and exercises aren't a formula to be followed legalistically. Nonetheless, we urge you to give the process a try, using the full instructions for each exercise and checklist.

This will encourage you to stay close to the Bible. It will keep you going back to the text to check your perceptions, your memory, and your impressions. It will also encourage you to stay close to yourself. It will help you become aware of what's going on in your life as you work with the text on your own and with other people. In short, following the exercises will help you resist the tendency to hide either from the Bible or from yourself.

But there is yet another benefit. These exercises are about the simple, everyday disciplines that go into friendship. Not just friendship with the Bible, but friendship with each other and with God. Friendship worked out in the context of life's ups and downs, gains and losses, sorrow and joy.

The exercises are about taking time to be together, thinking things over, asking productive questions, listening with an open mind, sharing your own point of view, paying attention to little things, being willing to change, admitting when you're wrong, respecting differences, including others in the circle, and counting on God's daily presence.

The disciplines of friendship aren't magical. But they can become a means of grace. They can contribute to the healing of old wounds, and to the support of new life. This won't happen simply because you follow the exercises dutifully. Rather, it will happen because God still loves to surprise us, using the small, seemingly insignificant, and even somewhat obsessive things of this world.

The Authors

Elouise Renich Fraser is professor of systematic theology at Eastern Baptist Theological Seminary in Philadelphia. Renich Fraser received a B.A. in biblical studies from Columbia Bible College (S.C.). She earned an M.A. in biblical studies and theology at Fuller Theological Seminary (Pasadena), and holds a Ph.D. in theology from Vanderbilt University (Nashville).

Renich Fraser has been active in the church since childhood. She is currently a member of Gladwyne Presbyterian Church (USA) in Gladwyne, Pennsylvania. She is a teacher, preacher, and church musician. Many of her speaking engagements are church-related, inviting people to experience for themselves how theological reflection serves the church. Topics of special interest include biblical interpretation, the difference God makes in human relationships, and the connections between everyday life and theology.

Renich Fraser has taught at Eastern Baptist Theological

Seminary since 1983. In addition to systematic theology, she teaches such courses as narrative theology, women's theologies in context, and images of Jesus. Areas of academic interest include Christology, the doctrine of humanity, Scripture, and spirituality. Her writings have appeared in scholarly and church-related publications. She is a member of the American Academy of Religion and the Karl Barth Society of North America.

Renich Fraser was born in Charlotte, North Carolina. She grew up in Seattle, Los Angeles, and Savannah (Ga.). Her husband, David, is professor of sociology and chair of the biblical and theological studies department at Eastern College in St. Davids, Pennsylvania. They have two adult children, Scott and Sherry.

Louis Kilgore is a family person with a pastor's heart. He has lived all his life in the U.S. metropolitan northeast. His family roots are in the farming area of southern York county, Pennsylvania. Louis grew and went to school mostly in New Jersey.

His whole life has been shaped by the Bible and the church community. He was raised in a Christian home with five brothers and one sister. His father is a retired pastor.

Louis worked for a while in the theater arts and education after graduation from Grove City College, Pa., where he received an A.B. in Religion/Philosophy. In 1983, he married Betsy Baker and enrolled at Eastern Baptist Theological Seminary. He graduated with a M.Div. in 1986 and was ordained by the New Brunswick Presbytery (N.J.) in 1993. Louis and Betsy have four children: Gregory, Gretchen, Megan and Emily, and worship at the First Presbyterian Church (USA) of Ewing, New Jersey, where Louis is associate pastor. Louis is a lively preacher who enjoys growing and learning with other people.